The Body & The Cosmos

Exploring The Astrological, Philosophical, and

Physical Connection

By Nadiya Shah

Dedicated to my Fabulous Friends, Fans, Superstars,

and Students. Thank You for seeing me as a part of

your sacred journey, as you are part of mine.

I am grateful.

Table of Contents

Introduction

There is beauty, power, magic, acceptance and love that can be found in experiencing your spirit infused in the matter that is the physical body. It is perhaps the greatest blessing of being human. We are both consciousness and physical beings, experienced in unison.

I might hear remarks like, "I am not my body." To claim so is to deny us the amazing opportunity that exists in knowing one's self more deeply through the experience of being embodied. We do not simply understand the world through our mind, but we are always actively engaged in perceiving information and gaining knowledge through a variety of physical senses. Our bodies perceive and process knowledge and experiences. Our mind is a part of this process.

Over-identification with the body creates distortion as well. This creates a situation where we begin to identify with a part of us that is ultimately false. To place undue importance on the appearance is unsatisfying because the appearance is temporal, subject in some ways to the winds of influences like genetics, external events, and age. Once undue importance is placed on appearances above the spiritual experience of being in the body, we have moved away from being embodied and understanding the body as a site and source of wisdom.

To see yourself only from the outside is to disregard the experience that comes from within. There is something to be said for focusing your attention on the information coming in through the senses; how you witness the world from the place of being in a physical body. To care more about how you are being perceived by others and placing prominence on how you look takes away the power of the spiritual experience of being alive. The power of being a human being is gone.

In this situation there is no embodiment, only insecurity and uncertainty. There is also no authentic self-love in this situation. If you think that in order to be loved we need to look a certain way or be physically appealing to others, you have moved out of the body and out of love, for the love you seek from the world is not within. You are denying yourself of the acceptance you crave.

Acceptance is one of the greatest experiences of embodiment.

Self-image is one thing, but the experience of being active and being alive is another completely different spiritual reality. Being alive is a powerful spiritual experience, free from the emotionally fluctuating perception of self-image. Being alive is breath, wonder, centeredness, balance, beauty, strength, renewal, constant change, inner transformation and feeling the power of spirit. It returns one to one's self. It becomes a grand microcosm within your own body for how the entirety of the Universe, and all of the beautiful spiritual lessons contained within and through it, exists within your individual being. It is transcendence to feel the spirit through the body and know that it is in every part of you and yet you are bigger. It is life. And life is a great gift.

I have also heard people say that God isn't somewhere outside; God is within us. There is nothing like experiencing your body as alive through being physically active that the God-force itself comes to the foremost. It is God itself that is experienced through physical activity, not by divorcing one's self from the body. It is by recognizing and experiencing wisdom and knowledge through the perspective of having a body, not just a mind, that we claim to be embodied. It is to experience spirit and body as one.

There have been some benefits stemming from divorcing the mind and body. People are recognized as inherently spiritual. Most people have had the experience, whether through disease or injury, when an interesting dichotomy presents itself. Those are times when we feel that our spirit wants one thing, but the demands of our body require something else. Changes in the body, or an unhealthy state, can sometimes indicate when we are living a life out of balance or in some way inauthentic to ourselves. However, this isn't usually the case. We think that our body needs changing based on how it appears. There are times when we feel powerless over our body, and therefore ourselves. Times when our body does not behave as we would like it to, or isn't expressing what we view ourselves to be, or when we feel a deadweight weighing us down, a weight that feels burdensome and impeding. In these cases, we can be caught in a strange duality, feeling a separation, while still seeking to gain some knowledge, some power, which will allow resolution and unity. These are the times when the spiritual lesson of acceptance makes itself most known.

There is certainly a part of us that is experienced independent of the body, an awareness that lets us know that there is consciousness within us. But we are in bodies right now and experience this consciousness through the body. It is because we have bodies that certain phrases or images can give us chills, raise our heartbeat, or leave us breathless. It is because we are essentially embodied that we can know our experience to be a spiritual one, because it is by knowing the spirit infused in the body that we come to gain knowledge and have moments of absolute wonder.

The tree does not inspire us only because it is a physical presence. Nor does it inspire simply because there is something that is not the tree that is denoted by its presence. The tree, the flower, and other aspects of the natural environment have the power to move us because they speak to the merging of spirit and matter. They are infused with spirit. They indicate something sacred because they exist in the physical form, not in spite of it.

The famous quote "I am a spiritual being having an earthly experience" holds two parts to an equation. It is acknowledging the sacred expression that we are, and also that this sacredness is experienced in the present moment, in and through our earthly, embodied experience. We are not purely spiritual beings in the same sense that a spirit or angel might be. We have physical bodies that are a part of our spirituality, a part of our spiritual existence. It is because of the body that we know we have emotions, desires, and spiritual lessons. It is because of the body that we can know ourselves as sacred. It is because of the body that we can even have a mystical experience, for it is the senses that become altered and heightened during such events in the spiritual life of the human being.

The Mind-Body-Soul connection speaks to this, though not overtly. Because the Mind is placed first, there is the recognition that we do have an aspect of us that is experienced as autonomous and individualistic. The Mind makes conscious decisions and can guide the Body in the direction it desires to go. The Body is recognized as intelligent, as a part of this connection. It does not operate independently of the Mind and the Soul. In fact, the Body is infused with Soul, and guided and informed by the Mind. This infusion, for me, is the most important and also most disconnected to how we understand this connection. The Body has a wisdom and knowledge that is all its own. It stands witness in love and non-judgment, to all the things we feel and all that we think. The Soul permeates us all, yet we have an individual Soul that speaks to the depths of our desires and yearning.

The Sufis say that the Universe is in a place of continuous unfolding, gradually revealing itself to us. In the same way, the intricacy of our Mind-Body-Soul connection is also a place of constant revelation. The more deeply we understand just what the Mind-Body-Soul connection means to each of us in our own lives, the more we will come to know ourselves better.

To know ourselves better, as an integrated whole, yet connected to everyone and everything. This is perhaps one of the greatest freedoms.

Defining Spirituality

To define spirituality is a daunting task, because it is so highly relative. What I consider spiritual is closely aligned with what I consider truth. Defining truth is deeply personal. I am certainly influenced by New Age philosophy, with its emphasis on inner authority. In fact, I do believe that it is in the voice of inner authority that we find the divine.

Deciphering between fears and the divine guidance from within can be difficult sometimes until I ask myself two key questions:

does knowing this or believing this make me a kinder person? Does this move me closer to love? These two key questions, centered on kindness and love, are my barometer as to whether something I feel is rooted in fear or God. If I am not moving closer to kindness or love, then it is most likely fear that is motivating my actions, or the lens with which I am justifying them.

Another distinction that is valuable for me is separating religion from spirituality. In its most positive understanding, religion is a place of community, cultural identity, and altruism. What I am discussing in this book is separate from these things. Spirituality is the personal cultivation of an enhanced union with one's own creator, interchangeably called God, Universe, Source, Higher Power or Higher Self.

Throughout history it was understood that what was in our external world was also a part of us within. The Sufi Ibn'Arabi considered the human body a microcosm to the macrocosm that is the Universe. The human body is, in its entirety, not only a complete reflection of the Universe, but also connected to and contains the Universe, right down to each of its intricate parts. Through this exploration we can begin to consider our physical self symbolically, revealing our emotional lessons and spiritual truths, especially in times of discomfort or pain.

As our human understanding about ourselves and our world has evolved, so too has our understanding of the cosmos and our connection to it. The sky is now seen as exemplified archetypes, denoting our collective and individual experience. Every one of these 12 archetypes is an aspect of all of us, although as we explore, we will find ourselves resonating with some more strongly than others, given our personal tendencies and history. Through the Neo-Platonic rationale called "sympathy," every single aspect of the lived world, human reality, right down to the different parts of our body, was divided into the separate domain of each of the 12 archetypes. The varying nature of each part of the body reflects and symbolizes aspects of the soul and our shared human experiences.

What This Book Is and What It Isn't

This work was inspired by researching Plato's "Timaeus," in which he describes his theory of sympathy, and our mystical understanding of our connection to the cosmos, held together by "vital chains." The personal and astrological correspondences I made from there are detailed in this book. Because of the focused nature of this book, exploring the zodiac from the perspective of its connections to the different parts of the human body, students of medical astrology may find it useful. Others who are interested in deepening their personal connection to the cosmos may also find inspiration in connecting their embodiment with the sky. However, for a more encompassing introduction, have a look at my book "Astrology Realized," which provides an introduction to Natal Chart Astrology.

This book in no way provides medical advice, or suggests explicitly or implicitly, that there is any medical advice herein. Personally, I have found tremendous benefit from consulting medical doctors and using established medical treatment, including medications. If you have any symptoms that could use the advice, insight, or opinion of a doctor, please do consult with your doctor as soon as possible. Medical professionals are here for a reason, as part of practical measures we can take to bring balance to spirit and matter. Doctors are doing sacred work, as part of continuing a sacred tradition of healing, in a modern context. For this, and the ways in which doctors and other medical professionals have helped me, members of my family, and other people I love, I am personally forever grateful.

Another point of clarity; I do not believe that we necessarily manifest our physical ailments. There are times when we are genuinely powerless in the face of physical pain and challenge. However, I do believe that any feeling, ailment, emotion, or experience, no matter how challenging, can be learned from and learned through. I do believe that there is a higher wisdom playing out in all things, even if we can't recognize it or appreciate it in the moment. I do believe that we can take any challenge, physical or otherwise, and use it as an opportunity to become more loving and wiser than we were before.

However, sometimes the wisdom is to connect with medical professionals. As part of the intricate tapestry of our lives, in connecting with others, in being in certain spaces, we can't always know on the surface how many infinite possibilities are opened to us. Even if our physical distress is not ideal, and something we hope for is fleeting, in seeking help, we may open ourselves to experiences, connections with people, and inner wisdom that might not have been possible any other way.

I consider this book to be partly contemplative, and partly proactive. The contemplative part allows you to consider the sky and its connection to you more personally than you have before. The proactive part includes specific actions you can take, from physical activities to meditative focus, that can help you cultivate your unique relationship with the cosmos.

Each chapter is divided into 2 main sections. The Body and The Cosmos is part exploration, part meditation. The section where we focus on the body includes a contemplation on our physical connection to the sky. Here you will see specific traditional exercises and yoga poses you can incorporate as part of your workout or other health routines, to affirm your connection to the cosmos through that part of your body, linked to another part of the zodiac.

The second section features an outline of meditations you can practice. First, you'll learn some basics of breath, and then learn a few techniques per sign, to help in your meditative explorations on your connection to the cosmos.

How To Use This Book

You'll notice that each sign of the first section begins with correspondences. Specific colors, semi-precious stones, flowers or herbs are included in this list. As part of your explorations on your connection to the sky, you may wish to incorporate some of these external correspondences to your routines, meditations, or rituals as a means to strengthen the physical and spiritual qualities that sign represents. Just like Plato's theory of Sympathy correlates the body to the sky, so does all of our physical world around us. These correspondences encourage you to align your immediate environment with the actions you take, whether those actions are physical steps or intentional spiritual alignment.

You may choose to time your practices, whether meditative or otherwise, in accordance to moon cycles, new moons or full moons, or perhaps the solar cycles, delving into a sign of an astrological month. Others might want to focus only on the suggestions for the moon sign, rising sign, or sun sign as part of utilizing these suggestions. Regardless of how you first incorporate the information in this book, my hope is that you know that this wisdom is always here, available to you. Just as the entirety of the cosmos is a part of you as well, so will the potential benefit of each of the signs and sections be here for you to develop and grow too.

I do believe that the singular thing any astrologer can do to help themselves be as good an astrologer as possible, is to cultivate a personal relationship with the astrological sky. All its symbols, planets, asteroids, stars, and constellations represent an intimate connection that connects deep within you. We are made of the same stuff as the stars, after all. The more you cultivate this relationship between all of yourself and more of the sky, the more they will be able to speak to you personally. The more it is also that they will be able to speak through you personally, as you interpret their symbols. Interpretation is the defining act of being an astrologer. You will be able to speak to the sky with greater richness and conviction the more you cultivate this relationship through your time in contemplation, education, and experiential meditation.

What I do hope is to encourage your contemplation on the sacredness of the body and its integration with the cosmos. I hope to remind us that our bodies and our lives are part of a magnificent and divine expression, as glimpsed in the mystery of the sky which we are intimately connected to.

Meditation and The Cosmos

If you haven't done it before, it may seem like a remote concept, done only by Buddhists in a monastery somewhere isolated and far away, living in a different reality than you do. Sure, they have their way of mediating that works for them, and I am sure that after meditating for 30 years, those far away mystics have seen their practice grow, change, and enhance. If you choose to make meditation a part of your spiritual practice, and I think it's a great idea if you do, then you too will see your practice be enhanced the more you practice it. This has been proven true for me and many, many others.

The reason I emphasize meditation in this book is because it is one of the most immediate ways to explore your connection to the sky. It is meditation that connects all the information in this book. It turns the philosophies presented here, and translates them into lived experience. An experience that will be intimately all your own.

Mediation is simply focusing your attention. That's all. We choose to focus our attention on different things all the time. But when we meditate, we choose to be aware of what we are focusing our attention on—and choosing to focus our attention on something that will in some way empower us mentally, emotionally, or spiritually.

The easiest way to introduce yourself to meditation is to focus on your breath for a few moments. I've heard more than one yoga enthusiast say that the Breath is the bridge between the body and mind. The breath is our connection with the divine. The breath is our connection to our bodies and ourselves. The breath is our connection with being human. The breath is healing. Breathing is spiritual. Breathing is essential. Breathing can make you high. Breathing can ground you.

Experiment with your breath. It can be an enlightening and rewarding experience, and it is right there waiting for you.

I will first introduce you to the power of paying attention to your breath. You will do some variety of this meditation at the start of each of the meditations by sign. It is in this practice of breathing, that you will put yourself into a meditative state, enough to become more receptive to the astrological sign meditation at hand, and therefore reap its full benefits.

At first, the process of attention to breath will be deliberate. You will be experimenting to find your unique way to calm and center yourself. Allow yourself to experiment and get comfortable with these fist exercises. Once we move on to each sign, you'll find this time you took to be comfortable with your breath to be as tremendously valuable in your journey.

Once we get to the meditations by sign, you will find I begin and end each meditation the same way. That is to remind you of the power of breath and intention, as you begin your practice. I do this so that each section can be considered as a whole, and can guide you fully through each sign of the cosmos within.

The specific technique used once we get to the signs can be considered a guided visualization, in that I will direct your focus and imagination towards the correspondences related to that sign. Your mind will begin to move away from the passive awareness of breath, and towards a more active receptivity. You are using your imagination, that's the active part. But you will also be open to discovering the wisdom your imagination takes you to.

As you prepare to take part in meditation, make sure you first have a quiet, uninterrupted space where you feel safe to close your eyes and focus completely on the task at hand. Once you have demarcated your space, be sure to gather your correspondences. This will include some of the colors, herbs, semi-precious and precious stones, or flowers. You can find a short list of some of these correspondences in the previous section, The Body and The Cosmos. There, you will find each sign begins with a few items that will encourage you to consider how the entire cosmos is infused in all aspects of matter, our physical world. This is by no means anywhere near an exhaustive list. Additionally, make sure you have a notebook or other recording device of your preference nearby, to jot down any insights or ideas that may be valuable to you, as part of your meditation journey for this day.

Once you know the space you will meditate in, I would invite you to consider what correspondences you could bring in. Consider indulging your senses. You might consider lighting incense, comprised of the herbs and flowers that correspond with the sign you want to focus on for this meditation. This will engage your sense of smell and breath. You might also consider holding one of the stones that fits the correspondence or having it in front of you within your meditation's space. You might also light a candle in one of the colors associated with the sign you will work with for this meditation. I will invite you to be creative, and consider your options, as part of creating a space that will encourage you to connect with your astrological sky.

As you move through the visualizations outlined here, take your time on each of the steps. Ensure that you are deeply feeling each of the visualizations before you move on to the next one.

Whatever image or feeling comes, allow it to surface. Don't judge it. Allow it to come forward without expectation. Make note of what you see, feel, and experience, knowing that this is the way in which wisdom is speaking to you at this moment. This way, you will stay focused and you'll make the most of this time with yourself and your astrological sky.

Introduction to Breath:

Lie down or sit in a comfortable position. Close your eyes. You might want to place your hands on your diaphragm just under your rib cage, or anywhere else that allows you to further observe your process of breath. Start to pay attention to your breathing. Don't control it in any way yet, just pay attention to how you are breathing. Feel the breath move through your face, your nose, your mouth, fill your brain and move deeper into your body.

Is your breath reaching all the way down into your diaphragm? How low does it go? Does it all stay in your upper chest? How high does your breath go? Are you a fast breather or a slow breather? Just observe your breathing pattern and habits for a moment.

When you're ready, start a breathing pattern that goes like this; take in a deep slow breath for 3 counts, and then exhale for 3 counts/seconds. Try that a few times before changing the breathing pattern to something like this: take a deep breath in on the count of 3. Hold that breath for 3 seconds, then exhale for 3 seconds, and then let your lungs be empty for 3 seconds. Lather, rinse, then repeat. Do this a few times, like a rhythmic, circular motion.

When you're ready, increase the count to 4. So, your breathing rhythm will go like this: inhale for 4 seconds, hold for 4, exhale 4, hold empty for 4, and repeat. Do this a few times and get comfortable with it.

When you are ready, increase your count to 5. Follow the same deep rhythmic breathing style. Try and get your breath in your body as deep as possible. Focus only on your breath and how it feels going in, staying in, and leaving your body. If your thoughts wander, no worries. Just lovingly bring them back to your breath.

When you are ready, increase the count to 6.

When you are ready, increase the count to 7.

Take it slow and deep, and allow yourself to really connect with your breath to the best of your ability.

Ok, 7 is as high as we are going to go for now! Unless you want to take it higher and deeper. The choice is yours.

When you feel like you have explored your breath enough for now, then stop focusing on it. Just gently bring your attention to your eyes and open them when you are ready. Slowly bring your attention back to the physical world

How do you feel? What was that like for you?

When I first did this exercise, I was amazed at how HIGH I felt. All that oxygen really got me buzzing. It took my body a while to get used to actually giving it the oxygen it needed. The other thing that made an impression is how my mind calmed down the more I focused. This exercise allowed me to calm down mentally and emotionally. The more I did this, the less my mind would wander. And when it did wander, I just loving brought it back to my breath.

This practice of deep breathing is foundational to knowing the cosmos within your body. It is through breath that we learn to still our mind long enough to hear our most important wisdom.

It is through allowing my mind to be calm and relaxing my body that I was able to utilize and benefit from other meditations that are more guided and focused on gaining access to the wisdom and love of the astrological sky. You too can benefit from all the other meditations in this book and other books you read by practicing deep meditative breathing.

The Body and The Cosmos

Throughout history it was understood that what existed in our external world was also a part of us within. Mythological tales and attributes were ascribed to different segments of the sky, outlining how parts of the sky, and all of it in its entirety, were intimately connected to a part of us emotionally and spiritually.

As our human understanding about ourselves and our world has evolved, so too has our understanding of the cosmos and our connection to it. The sky is now seen as exemplified archetypes, denoting our collective and individual experience. Every one of these 12 archetypes is an aspect of all of us, though as we explore, we will find ourselves resonating with some more strongly than others, given our personal tendencies and history. Through the Neo-Platonic rationale called "sympathy," every single aspect of the lived world and human reality, right down to the different parts of our body, was divided into the separate domain of each of the 12 zodiacal signs. This chapter will explore the astrological myths that tell us about the varying natures of each part of the body, as it reflects the soul.

Learning from our external environment and attempting to make a judgment as to the consequences before we undertake action is not a new or strictly astrological phenomenon. We all do this, in various ways, every day. When I wake up and look out my window, I begin to ascertain what the indications reveal about the likely changes in weather. This is one small example of how I am constantly seeking to learn from my external environment and what it has previously told me about the consequences of many possible actions.

This willingness to understand myself as a part of the world, not some random isolated mind tied to a body, but rather a being that is alive, learning, and spiritually receptive while remaining a positive force of change and consequence, lays the philosophical and spiritual foundation with which I approach my own life, the life of others, and the world at large.

This philosophical position is an understanding that what is outside of us, what is in the external environment, is symbolic of what is within us. This idea originates in the western world from Plato's "Timaeus," in which he articulates that an intelligent cosmos is personally connected to each one of us, to the intricacies of our physical body. The intelligence that is of the cosmos is akin to our own, and understanding the cosmos through observation brings wisdom and self-knowledge. This mystical understanding of the sky, echoed in the work of later Neo-Platonists like Plotinus, and many mystics including Ibn'Arabi, holds that the entire Universe is symbolic of how we are, how we operate, and what we feel. As such, the entirety of the sky is within us.

Everything in our lived experiences to any physical discomfort we may have is an opportunity to understand ourselves more deeply, if we are willing to look at it symbolically. This does not mean that if medical matters arise that we should not seek the help that we need. A part of self-care is knowing when to ask for help. In addition, to accept the help we need, especially in times of a medical emergency or when our lives are on the line is a deeply personal and incredibly intelligent decision. However, while we are going through a health challenge, or simply some discomfort, or even a process of self-discovery, it may be helpful to consider what is going on in the larger perspective.

I do believe the entire Universe conspires on our behalf; all to help us learn and grow in the direction our soul desires to go. Plato has said in the "Timaeus" that to contemplate the cosmos is to cultivate wisdom, and that is the point of life. To consider it symbolically and esoterically means that we garner the most benefit we can from the situation. It means that no matter how trying, testing, or annoying some physical ailment may be, contemplating the emotional and spiritual implications means that we compare the experiences we are having with how our body feels as part of the process of becoming wiser. In this way, no matter what happens, no matter how deep the uncertainty of our personal situation may be, something there allows us to cultivate some self-knowledge, some wisdom, which gives way to our own truth.

The entirety of the cosmos is within us. All the astrological symbols utilized here are within us too. Each segment of the sky rules a different segment of the body. Below are my thoughts on each of these parts and their esoteric relevance. It is meant to be a starting point, to facilitate a deep connection to a cosmos you can feel within. It is also meant to be a meditation so that each of us can begin here, or return to when a particular part of the body is calling on us for attention, and be led to a meditation of our own. In this way, we can come to conclusions that speak to a truth that is all our own. The astrological mythologies are associated with celestial symbols, each deeply connected to our spiritual and therefore physical being. They need to be thought of as contained within us, and each one of these energies desire cultivation and attention. To ignore any sign, regardless of what your sun sign is and what it says about who you get along with or who you do not, is to ignore a part of ourselves.

The one thing that is recurrent in my own physical challenges is that when some part of my body is distressed, it is usually because somewhere in my life, the way I am using my energy is out of balance. I do what I can to try and restore this balance. I will be diligent in some cases, depending on the severity of the inconvenience. Nevertheless, there comes a point where surrender is required. That surrender makes new answers possible. The acceptance that things are as they are, the willingness to do all I can, and then the surrender and faith it takes to let go of all I cannot control. Once surrender happens, new information can come in. Information that allows me to glimpse the immensity and mystery of a higher plan for my life, a plan beyond any goal or vision I could hold for myself.

I have also utilized these understandings during the course of my workouts. I have contemplated the detail of each muscle, and as I developed it, I focused on how I was growing emotionally, spiritually, and on the life skills I was acquiring as well. I have included some of these understandings, and in some cases, specific exercises, that help strengthen me in ways that are less superficial, more esoteric. As the muscle is worked, I focused on what was building within me emotionally. I have chosen to share some specific exercises so that you can see how utilizing these and developing a specific muscle could be a part of your own unique spiritual exploration. The physical body is a symbol, a deeply personal symbol as to what is going on in other energetic levels. What happens on mental, emotional, and spiritual levels of our lives must show in the physical. Ultimately, it is a deeply personal judgment, to see what our body and weight is trying to tell us about ourselves. The exercises suggested or indicated here, and what they will mean to you, what awareness they bring and what they strengthen, is a deeply personal process that is all your own.

However, it is simultaneously important to hold non-judgment in the same space as curiosity and open-mindedness. However we look to others, it is not up to us to judge them based on their physical condition. It is not even up to us to judge ourselves. Rather, if we can instead strive to see the perfection in all things, including our current physical state, we might start to glimpse the wisdom of this very moment and exactly how we feel right now.

The information that is presented originates from the ancient medical system known as *iatromathematics*. In the Renaissance and earlier periods, it was common practice for a medical practitioner to have a familiarity of the planets. In fact, astrological education and techniques were regular aspects of assessment. It is important to note here that people during this time had a certain frame of mind that might be foreign to many people today. All sciences were inherently spiritualized. Scientific knowledge, in any field, including medicine, could not and was not held as separate from its symbolic, spiritual significance. There are artifacts that can be found in many museums that speak to these practices, with devices that could be used to calculate a person's planetary birth chart on the spot during the doctor's visit.

The doctors of the time would use astrology to aid in an accurate diagnosis by considering not only the symptoms that the patient was exhibiting, but also by predicting what that person's birth

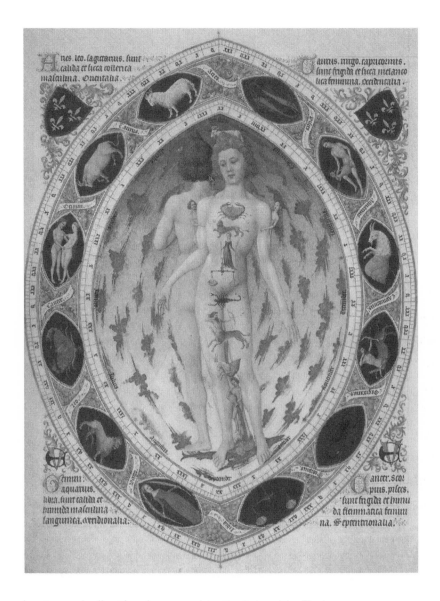

chart was indicating in regard to their health. Today, we understand our free will and agency differently than in more fatalistic times. While making predictions is controversial in our modern times, considering our physical symptoms in line with the psychological and spiritual opportunities they present allows to utilize our free will, and it also modernizes ancient knowledge to our benefit. Though the information presented here is not nearly as detailed as what these practitioners would utilize, it is in some ways inspired by their work and considered within a contemporary framework.

Ultimately this became a highly relative inquiry. It literally involved paying attention to what was happening with me emotionally, what thought patterns were swimming in my head whenever I felt something taking place physically. I did not realize it at the time, but I was creating a bond with my body, allowing its aches and pains to speak to me symbolically. The associations I made were ultimately not a part of any tradition, though certainly influenced by my inquiries into them. The conclusions I made spoke mainly to what revealed itself as relevant for me.

It may be helpful to consider the parts of the body that each constellation represents and then look to the spiritual and emotional attributes. Where this aspect of spirit is not being fully expressed, it can manifest in the physical body corresponding to that part of the spirit. For example, I have learned that whenever my eyes feel itchy, it is usually some aspect of Aries energy, some part of taking ownership for what I see and having the faith to start those initiatives in need of my attention. It is important to understand how each of the constellations relates to some spiritual expression, and thus those expressions found in different areas of the body.

The following is a systematic look into the body. Masculine and feminine, as principles, are a part of us all, and find their expression in our physical and spiritual being. The elements were believed by Plato to comprise the entire Universe, and everything contained within, including us. The elements are the foundation to which we are built. Each has a function and significance that permeate out lives. It is important to recognize and find the balance of these symbols, and what they represent, if we are to be balanced people. Finally, each of the twelve archetypes, sorted in the division of the body, from top to bottom, will be explored.

Masculine and Feminine.

Like ying and yang, the perception holds that all the world's energies are either masculine, feminine, or in some rare cases, neutral. This is not about the actual gender, rather, it is about the qualities of receptivity associated with the feminine as a principal and actions that are associated with the masculine when understood as a principal. We all have both these energies within us. When there is an imbalance in my body, the first place I look is to see if these energies are imbalanced, if one is being more cultivated than the other.

The right brain and eye, and the entire left side of the body are feminine. The left brain and eye, and the entire right side of the body are masculine. When someone is experiencing problems on one of these sides, especially when they are troubled in several places, it usually indicates an imbalance of energy.

If it is the right side, then it is usually a feeling that action is not being taken or not taking place that is the culprit. Somewhere in our lives, we feel that things are not transpiring the way we desire, or that we are not taking the type of power and agency over our lives, or in the events in our lives, that we desire. The right side has to do with taking initiative and purposeful action on our own behalf. A good mantra to affirm and balance this energy is: "Everything is taking place as it should. I can take action on my own behalf. I am strong and capable."

If it is the left side, then it has to do with our feminine energy; this is intuition and receptivity. So, in some way, we might not be listening to the promptings of the Universe or otherwise not listening to our inner voice. Problems in our body are asking us to be more receptive and open, find a source of insight and understanding, and also, to just take a break to develop a greater appreciation of what our lives already are. The left side has to do with acceptance. The mantra used to cultivate and balance feminine energy would be "I listen to life, acknowledge what I feel, and go with the flow."

The Elements

The entire Universe was said to be divided into four elements. Fire and air, which are masculine, and earth and water, which are feminine. Ether, the fifth element, can be considered the spirit that permeates all that is seen in the physical realm.

Fire

It provides heat at its best, and destruction at its worst. It can be blatant, passionate, forceful, confident, and certain. Courageous, creative, inspiring, and inspired. Too much fire is destructive, arrogant and bossy, but fire is needed, for without it there is no drive, ambition, or zeal for the gift of life. It is optimistic. Fire is often described as being a gift of the Gods because it grants some of the things that humanity has noted as its strengths- our creative ability to actualize and transform. Fire is undeniable. This truth is the fire of spirit, and it believes in the right for us all to shine. Fire is masculine, and therefore active. Those who are very connected to their own fire energy and identify with it strongly believe themselves to be special. It is the element of creative energy.

Think about fire. What does it do? It blows around, it is hard to contain, and its heat burns so bright it is irrefutable. Fire is exemplified in music with a strong beat or pulse. If this energy is not actively cultivated, it can feel restless very quickly. Fire is masculine and is action oriented, and to honor this part of you give yourself something to do, something to be excited about, something to motivate it. Without an active project or something to feel enthusiastic about, this part of us can turn in on itself and become very frustrated if allowed to stagnate. Anytime we allow ourselves lots of sun and warmth, we connect with our own fire.

Fire Signs are considered masculine and represent a principle of action.

Air

Air is the realm of thought, of intellect, and ideas that happen on the mental plane. It is inspired brilliance and genius, clever and idealistic. Too much and it is mad genius, erratic thoughts, and being wrapped up in one's thoughts. Too little and there is no rational thought or ability to step back and consider things from a more detached place. Communication, perception, invention, balance, and fairness are all characteristic of air. It is quick, changeable, and futuristic. Air is masculine, and therefore active. Listening to music that has positive, uplifting lyrics is one way to tap into and cultivate our own energy. This is the element of truth, as is fresh air and breathing deep. Air can be all over the place too, and so it needs discernment and rationality to balance it and make it work to our advantage.

Air Signs are considered masculine and represent a principle of progression.

Water

It flows, it changes, has depth that can barely be deciphered when you look at the surface. It picks things up as it goes along, including information. Water is therefore characteristic of intuition, emotion, deep feeling, psychic, compassionate and perceptive on emotional levels. Too much water washes reality out, but you need the right amount to live, find meaning in life and a connection to a more mystical "life force." Water is feminine and therefore receptive. Alcohol abuse is a characteristic of cultivating water in less conscious, or less than effective, ways. This is the element of feeling and emotions.

Some more balanced ways of cultivating this energy include spending time in water, either in a swimming pool or natural setting, like a beach or lake. Meditation, when undertaken to connect with our own creative force, also connects us with this part of ourselves. Anytime we feel something, hear our own intuition, or are willing to make a change in the moment, based on what "feels" most right, we are honoring our water energy.

Water signs are considered feminine and represent the principle of intuition.

Earth

The earth is sturdy, practical, planted, and grounded. It is the natural, and like nature, everything grows in its own time and has a process. Earth is the realm of the material and physical. It can be conservative in its realism. Too much earth can be very materialistic, thinking that what is accumulated is all that matters, but too little earth and nothing manifests in the physical realm. Like Mother Earth, she is feminine and therefore receptive.

Earth is cultivated in a few powerful ways. Eating grains is one way, as the grains themselves allow the earth to become assimilated into us. Taking walks in natural environments, especially those that are uncultivated and teeming with wildlife, becomes a living example of how manifestation occurs with perfection and wisdom. Gardening, and even walking barefoot in the grass, are some simple ways to connect with our own physicality. The fruits of cultivating this part of us includes the self-respect that comes from working diligently towards your desired outcomes and then seeing those outcomes manifest on the physical realm. This is the element of flesh and accomplishment.

Earth signs are considered feminine and represent the principle of practicality.

The next chapters will focus on the 12 archetypes and the body, as encapsulated by each of the signs of the zodiac. As we will be discussing specific muscles, it may be helpful to refer to this anatomical reference chart of the human musculature as you need going forward from here.

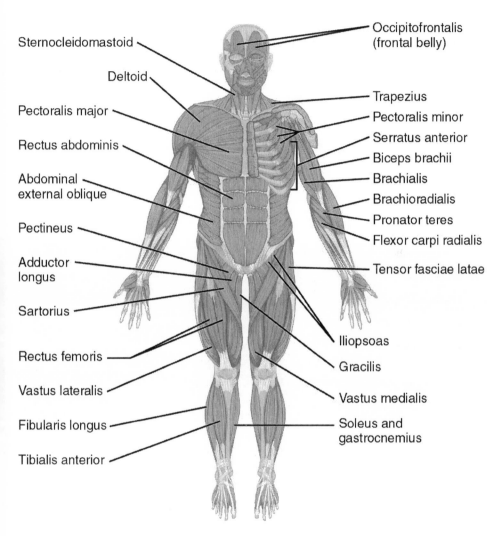

Sternocleidomastoid

Deltoid

Pectoralis major

Rectus abdominis

Abdominal external oblique

Pectineus

Adductor longus

Sartorius

Rectus femoris

Vastus lateralis

Fibularis longus

Tibialis anterior

Occipitofrontalis (frontal belly)

Trapezius

Pectoralis minor

Serratus anterior

Biceps brachii

Brachialis

Brachioradialis

Pronator teres

Flexor carpi radialis

Tensor fasciae latae

Iliopsoas

Gracilis

Vastus medialis

Soleus and gastrocnemius

Major muscles of the body.
Right side: superficial; left side:
deep (anterior view)

Aries

Athletic Endeavor, Spiritual Warrior, Harnessing the Will

Mars, Day

Fire Element

Ruby, Garnet, Bloodstone

Cinnamon, Pepper

Bright Red, Black, White, Gold

"I Own My Power"

This is the part of us that embodies fire and warmth, especially as a symbol of confidence and bold action. This is also the part of the cosmos that encapsulates the archetype of the warrior, the military, and the athlete for the bravery, power, and adrenaline rush. This is the "fire in the belly" we associate with those who are infused with a spirit or drive to make their mark and exert themselves on the world. This is also the energy of the entrepreneur, embodying the assured stance needed to trust your own ideas enough to bet they will be profitable. Like the Golden Fleece, there is something golden about this energy, something special that is shown to the world.

Aries energy is about going on in the world with confidence and a full sense of ownership of our ideas and worthiness to manifest them. Aries can be described as initiative full-on. The mantra is "I win." This is warrior, competitive energy. The spiritual warrior. Aries needs to have faith in itself, to trust its instincts, and start the thing that resonates most deeply with their core. It correlates to the parts of the body that are the skull, forehead, and eyes, and muscle structure in general.

My friend was complaining to me about headaches the other day. She said it was painful, throbbing, and extended at times into her eyes. I considered Aries, its spiritual and emotional qualities of initiation and confidence. I asked her if there was any area in which she felt like she was not starting, or taking some beginning action on her own behalf, or otherwise not showing trust in her instincts that were telling her what to start. She confirmed that she had not been applying for work, an action she knew she must take, as her current contract was nearing completion. I also asked her if there was some entrepreneurial action she desired to take but was resisting. She again confirmed that she had a strong desire to start her own agency, but did not see how she could do it, and had not even taken the initiating steps like researching the process, in order to begin the process. I also thought of the strong athletic and physical aspect denoted with this segment of the sky. True to the interpretation, she had also been ignoring her own sense of initiation, the one area of her life where she felt like she was taking care of herself and expressing her winning spirit.

This is also the part of the sky denoting the muscle structure. Our muscles are indicators of our strength; how much strength we can exert is sometimes dependent on their size. The more we can handle, the bigger they sometimes are. Strong muscles are associated with athletic excellence. Men, who are muscular, have an aura of safety around them. They are seen as being able to provide protection and consistency, perhaps speaking to the diligent and consistent exercise that is required to build them. Issues in the muscular structure can be centered on the ability to feel as though we are able to meet any challenge or provide safety and protection to ourselves and those closest to us.

Sometimes these areas covered by Aries can demand our attention when we do not trust our own "fire in the belly." This is when we have an intense desire to do something and yet are being held back by our fears. Problems with headaches in particular can be associated with self-criticism, because it is the lack of faith in our instinctual drives, and the fight against them, that can cause criticism to arise. This is not taking the action we know we should because we do not have the inherent belief that the prompting is wise. Ignoring certain prompts is to deny our worthiness to achieve what they may lead to, but more than that, it is to deny a useful and contented life, living true to that voice. Prioritizing is sometimes needed, but when we do what we tell ourselves we have to at the expense of what we desire to do, we create a conflict which can manifest in the body.

Our skull is comprised of a cranium, the encasing which protects our brain and the mandible (the jaw and lower bones of the face). Our skull acts as a shield protecting the very sensitive tissue of the brain and provides a framework for the face. Our skull is symbolic of our need to protect what we deem most vital, especially those things we think of as especially sensitive. The structural nature of the entire skull is symbolic of the structures to our identity, just as the face is the thing that most readily defines us.

Our forehead, as part of the skull, is the front part of the head. It provides protection as part of the skull, maintaining its symbol as shield, but also places the eyes, which deeply connects to the vitality of the soul.

The eyes are said to be the windows of the soul. Plato considered the eyes to be the very first organ that we are given, of all our physicality. Their purpose is to illuminate the soul, so that we may perceive things that would grant the soul wisdom. It is the soul, the truth of whom we are, our connection to our instincts and the confidence to take action in their support, that determination that can be evidenced in the eyes. Seeing our lives and ourselves with eyes that love ensures healthy, vibrant eyes. Having the faith and confidence in ourselves to be agents on our own behalf, and to take action in the direction that we most feel we desire to go, is a self-driven commitment that can be seen in our eyes. Our connection to energy, vitality and our own strength, combined with the willingness to explore its potential and the acceptance of its limitations, creates calmness in these eyes. These eyes, my eyes, resonate with an energy that harks to everything they have ever seen. My eyes are the windows to my soul. They can see the world from the perspective of the soul, and they also reveal when my soul is in a place of discontent. They are the most honest part of my face, and most honestly me. Aries also rules your hair. The mythologies of many cultures associated hair with strength. My hair, with its ability to constantly be shaped and shifted, speaks to the changes in my soul.

Exercises that develop this energy include raising the heart rate to the point of profuse sweating, like cardio exercises done in a rhythmic, continuous beat, with special emphasis on the kind of activities that take place outdoors in wild, natural settings with fresh air, like running or speed walking.

Yoga practices include Hot Yoga, as a general principal, to inspire sweat and engage the fire energy of this sign.

Meditation for Aries

Lie down or sit in a comfortable position. Close your eyes, or if you prefer, you can choose to start by softly gazing towards an image that feels calming to you. Start to pay attention to your breathing. Don't control it in any way yet, just pay attention to how you are breathing. Feel the breath move through your face, your nose, your mouth, fill your brain and move deeper into your body.

As you continue to breathe, begin to take your breath deeper. Take a few big breaths in. Feel the strength and power of your breath, filling you with energy and life. Feel your body rise and fall with each breath in. As your body relaxes more, you also can feel yourself more alert, as your mind fills with oxygen.

And as you continue to breathe, bring your attention to the exhale as well. Feel yourself releasing any thoughts of the past or the future. With each exhale, you release any feeling that is not part of this moment, right now. Observe the in and out of your breath. With each exhale you release, with each breath in, you feel more and more aware of this present moment. The present moment is truly all there is. The present moment is where the power is.

As you continue to breathe

Imagine the air around you as clear, white light. It feels calming, energizing, and refreshing.

On each inhale, you are breathing in this brilliant white light.

Imagine this light flooding through your breath, into your eyes, and through your cranium and skull. It brings with it a calming, energizing, and refreshing feeling of happiness to your mind.

And as you continue to breathe

Gently bring your attention to the refreshing, energizing qualities of this energy. Feel this energy join your circulatory system.

Now imagine this brilliant, energizing white light flood through your body, circulating with your blood, filling each of your cells with this calming, energizing, and refreshing energy. Sit with this energy for a moment.

As you continue to breathe

Now gently bring your attention to your mantra for this meditation:

"I trust what I enjoy."

"I trust my first instincts."

"I breathe, I am, I begin."

Repeat these words to yourself. Feel these words merge with the bright white light, this calming, energizing, and refreshing energy flowing within you.

Once you feel yourself connected to these words, and as you continue to breathe, gently bring your attention to your eyes. With your eyes closed, an image begins to appear in the distance. It is an image of something that you feel yourself to be. Something that you desire to begin. Let it come to you slowly and gently. Don't force or judge the image. Just let it appear as it does. As you move closer to the image, you can feel yourself growing in excitement and happiness. You know you are on the right track. You know you are on the correct path. As you move closer, you feel the increasing joy of a child, in childlike wonder and play.

See yourself move right up to the image. You are directly in front of this inspired, joyous version of yourself. Immersed in an activity that feels like play to you. Allow yourself to be in this moment of play, enjoying each moment. Sit here for a moment, indulging this pure moment of joy.

As you continue to breathe

Feel yourself filled with gratitude, for whatever insight has presented itself to you. Whatever vision, whatever feeling. Affirm within you that there is wisdom in this exact moment. Give this other version of yourself a big hug, filled with love and gratitude. Know that this person is always there, always a part of you.

As you continue to breathe

See yourself get up and begin to step away, gently at first. You are moving away, but you continue to feel the connection and the gratitude move through you. Continue to feel yourself walk back, towards your awareness of your breath.

As you continue to breathe

Bring your attention gently to your breath. The feeling of your breath moving through your nose, your face, and your mouth.

Gently, as you connect more strongly to breath, bring your attention to your eyes. Give them thanks for all they are, all they have seen, and all they do.

As you continue to breathe

Gently feel yourself being in this present moment more and more. Begin to move your fingers and toes, with an awareness of the parts of your body in contact with a surface.

As you continue to breathe

Come back into this moment, and gently, as you are ready, open your eyes.

As you come back into this moment, and into your conscious awareness…

Jot down any thoughts that you'd like to affirm or remember in a notebook or recording device near you. And before you get up, be sure to thank this space that you were in, knowing that it was exactly as it needed to be.

Taurus

Money, Sensuality, Physical Enjoyment

Venus, Day

Earth Element

Emerald, Jade

Earth Colors, Greens

Red Roses

"I Enjoy My Journey Through Life"

This part of the sky is symbolic of sowing seeds in its early stages, with intelligence and an end goal in mind. As such, this is the archetype of putting the things into place with the assurance that a rich harvest will unfold later, as long as you follow the established procedure diligently and realistically. Earthly achievement on a steady path, thanking the earthly senses and the sensual pleasures of the earth along the way, again… and again, all contentedly fall under the sign of Taurus. This is the archetype of self-sufficiency, of knowing that we can take efforts to provide our needs and wants to ourselves. It is also the place that corresponds to our self-esteem and self-value, especially where it comes to building for ourselves materially.

The parts of the body that correlate with this part of the cosmos are the overall face, throat, neck, thyroid, voice, and the five senses. Its mantra is "I am worthy of accomplishment."

When I think about the face, I think of it as the part of myself that people see first. It is what I present to the world. The shape and structure of its entirety, but particularly of my nose, speak of my ancestry. My mouth is learning how to speak what is within me. This is perhaps a lifelong lesson. Our face, when not altered with cosmetic surgery, and in its most natural form, speaks most powerfully to our physical ancestry. When someone tells a parent their child looks just like him or her, they are usually referring to their face.

The overall face is what makes the most immediate impact when you meet others and is the most defining thing about us. As such, it represents how we feel about the impression we make on others. Our face is our first tool in building security and prosperity for ourselves, as part of the initial impression we make. It is what we bring to the table before we start to build skills to increase our prosperity.

The neck connects the wisdom of my body with the gift of discernment that my intellect provides. Yes, there is so much wisdom in the body that has been downplayed throughout history as being nothing more than the passions of the flesh that must be controlled. However, to think of that wisdom as only something that is working against us is to deny one of the most fundamental truths of human existence. "I think, therefore I am" is a popular philosophical assertion attributed to Rene Descartes. The intellect provides wonderful gifts and has granted rights in our modern era, when in contrast, ancient cultures would have had people killed or disowned for physical challenges. To rely solely on the intellect is to deny that we are holistic, integrated beings who hold wisdom that comes not only from careful thought and deliberation, but also from feeling. Feelings, emotions, and intuitive understanding all come from a deeper place and the intellectual mind. The neck thus represents our ability to communicate and eventually integrate these various places of knowledge.

The five senses fall under the archetype of Taurus because it is our senses that allow us undergo and enjoy our earthly experience. The mouth and nose, for their role among the five senses, are the parts of the body that connect to this archetype.

Our senses also speak to our level of presence. The more aware we are of the information being received by the five senses, the more we observe, the more we actually end up interacting with the external environment and its stimulants, and also with ourselves and how we process the variety of stimulation coming our way. Our senses are therefore a way of knowing our place in the world, in the present moment, and also within ourselves.

Our voice is symbolic of speaking our truth. The voice is created through folds found within the larynx, which is an organ. It is these folds that allow the richness and variety of sound to come forth from within us. This part of us symbolizes one of our most direct and earliest forms of self-expression, telling the world who we are. Demonstrating our sense of self-esteem. Anytime my throat hurts to the point where I can feel it when I speak, I know that in some way, what I am manifesting in my physicality is not in tandem with the esteem in which I hold myself. In addition, when I am not adapting to a change in my body or life that I know I am ready for, my resistance can show up with some discomfort in my voice.

The thyroid is a butterfly shaped gland that produces and regulates hormones that are imperative to the speed of our metabolism, that is, how much energy we burn. Put another way, the thyroid is directly involved in how quickly (or slowly) we process the food nourishment we ingest, how much of it we retain and how quickly we assimilate and release on an energetic, immediate level. The thyroid helps our body to create protein, a nutrient that contributes to the recovery and strength of our muscles. The thyroid is an endocrine gland, part of a system in our body that releases hormones directly into our blood. The hormones released by the thyroid are directly responsible for protein synthesis.

It is the role that the thyroid plays in synthesizing protein that powerfully symbolizes its role in making us stronger. Our willingness, or lack of it, to be stronger can be reflected in the health of the thyroid. What is also interesting is that a fast metabolism means there is more heat being generated by the body.

The thyroid is involved in a process that allows us to take what we ingest and allow it to make us stronger, better, making our nourishment a part of the earthly part of us, a part of our flesh. How willing we are to be nourished, and most significantly, be changed physically and materially as a result of nourishment, can be reflected in the health of the thyroid.

General voice exercises, that help us get in touch with the range of sound our voice can make, is one way to engage the archetype of Taurus through physical activity.

With yoga, the Bridge Pose can stimulate Taurus energy, through its emphasize on using the top parts of the body for balance.

Meditation for Taurus

Lie down or sit in a comfortable position. Close your eyes, or if you prefer, you can choose to start by softly gazing towards an image that feels calming to you. Start to pay attention to your breathing. Don't control it in any way yet, just pay attention to how you are breathing. Feel the breath move through your face, your nose, your mouth, fill your brain and move deeper into your body.

As you continue to breathe, begin to take your breath deeper. Take a few big breaths in. Feel the strength and power of your breath, filling you with energy and life. Feel your body rise and fall with each breath in. As your body relaxes more, you also can feel yourself more alert, as your mind fills with oxygen.

And as you continue to breathe, bring your attention to the exhale as well. Feel yourself releasing any thoughts of the past or the future. With each exhale, you release any feeling that is not part of this moment, right now. Observe the in and out of your breath. With each exhale you release, with each breath in, you feel more and more aware of this present moment. The present moment is truly all there is. The present moment is where the power is.

As you continue to breathe

Imagine the air around you as clear, vibrant, light pastel green colored light. Notice the shading and beauty of this light. It feels calming and grounding. It feels like an energy of love. This is the love of self. It is the light of the love that reminds you that who you are, exactly as you are, is perfect and worthy of this moment, celebrating yourself as you are right now.

Sit with this feeling of self love, being bathed in a feeling of absolute self acceptance.

On each inhale, you are breathing in this brilliant pastel light.

Imagine this light flooding through your breath, into your nose, and moving through each of your senses.

Slowly become aware of how this breath is being experienced through your sense of smell.

Now slowly become aware of how this breath is being experienced through your sense of taste.

Now slowly become aware of how this breath is being experienced through your sense of hearing.

Now slowly become aware of how this breath is being experienced through your sense of sight.

Now slowly become aware of how this breath is being experienced through your sense of touch.

And as you continue to breathe the clear, vibrant, light pastel green color around you

Gently bring your attention to the parts of your body that are in contact with the surface beneath you. It might be though your legs resting on a chair, or touching the ground beneath you. Perhaps your feet are on the ground. Gently feel yourself connected to the surface of the Earth. Supported by the Earth. Know that this support is always there.

Imagine yourself in a beautiful room. With your attention first on yourself, slowly, begin to look at the space around you. This room is filled with beautiful things, meaningful things. It is filled with what really matters. These might be personal or emotional qualities. Items with sentimental value. Or perhaps, you are in a room filled with all the material things you could ever want.

Everything in this room is just a glimpse into the abundance that is within you. And you being an expression of the Universe, it means that all these things are yours.

Spend a moment, sitting with the feeling of satisfaction, abundance, and contentment, knowing that all the things of the Universe are for you too.

Now gently bring your attention to your mantra for this meditation:

"My life Is a pleasure to experience."

"My life Is abundant."

"Divine love is self-love."

Repeat these words to yourself. Feel these words merge with the clear, vibrant, light pastel green color, this energy of self love, and the peace that it brings, flowing within you.

"My life Is a pleasure to experience."

"My life Is abundant."

"Divine love Is self-love."

As you continue to breathe

Feel yourself filled with gratitude, for whatever insight has presented itself to you. Whatever vision, whatever feeling. Affirm within you that there is wisdom in this exact moment.

Imagine yourself back in the room, and give yourself a big hug. A burst of your own love. Knowing that self love is the greatest abundance of all.

As you continue to breathe

See yourself turn your attention away from the room you have been in, and bring it back to you, gently at first. You are moving away, but you continue to feel the connection and the gratitude move through you. Continue to feel yourself turning your attention towards you, towards your awareness of your breath.

As you continue to breathe

Bring your attention gently to your breath. The feeling of your breath moving through your nose, your face, and your mouth.

Gently, as you connect more strongly to breath, bring your attention to your five senses. Give them thanks for all they are, all they have seen, touched, smelled, tasted, and heard, and all they do.

As you continue to breathe…

Gently feel yourself being in this present moment more and more. Begin to move your fingers and toes, with an awareness of the parts of your body in contact with a surface.

As you continue to breathe

Come back into this moment, and gently, as you are ready, open your eyes.

As you come back into this moment, and into your conscious awareness…

Jot down any thoughts that you'd like to affirm or remember in a notebook or recording device near you. And before you get up, be sure to thank this space that you were in, knowing that it was exactly as it needed to be.

Gemini

Writing, Speaking, Learning, Teaching, Media

Mercury, Day

Air Element

Topaz, Aquamarine, Turquoise

Parsley, Dill

White, Clear Green, Baby Blue

"I Express Myself Authentically"

Gemini rules the mind, thought, perception, and communication. As the symbol suggests, this is the sign of siblings, and thus getting along with others is important. This energy is very extroverted, symbolized by the part of us that desires to understand the world through communicating and sharing. That openness can give the appearance of confidence, but it is while being this way in the moment of honest mental exchange that self-consciousness leaves. There is a lot of mental energy here and the need for stimulation is high. This internal "busy-ness" also makes this energy the eternally youthful part of us.

Gemini is encapsulated in the image of the twins, which suggests separate parts of ourselves that understand the persona as distinct from the mind. Gemini, being an air aspect of ourselves, does rule mental function, but it also pertains with the concept of sharing in words, sharing of ourselves, spontaneously in the moment, and with trust in the process. It is through communicating that many of us come to know ourselves better. The duality of the twins is that there is a part of us that is shared and completely relatable, as a sibling would be. The world contains siblings and exemplifies the kind of open sharing that would take place among those in close quarters at a young age. This energy needs to feel that it is safe to freely express you as an individual, and learn in the process.

Questions that arise when this part of us asks for attention are: "Am I expressing myself the way that feels right to my heart?" "Am I being me?" "Am I talking enough?" "Am I sharing who I am?"

It is also the area where we process information on the mind level and make sense of our immediate environment by navigating it. There is no hint of self-consciousness with this energy, just free expression, which makes the persona appear confident.

However, with the inherent duality of this sign, there is also a desire to appear youthful and vigorous. This energy heals itself as it talks and any time we share honestly in words who we are and all we have experienced. It is a part of us that needs constant stimulation and has several things on the go simultaneously. Its nature is very quick, so it has the ability to multitask. The parts of the body this archetype correlates to are the nervous system, brain, lungs, shoulders, arms, and hands. The mantra is "I have to express to find my truth"

I was in my early twenties when I met Gloria, a movement teacher who offered classes in a small downtown room. I was, as many people at that young age can be, not certain of myself, my direction, or my life. However, I was willing to learn and explore, and so I found myself in Gloria's class. What I remember most about her class was that she would have us all hold resistance bands in both hands above our heads, and as we stretched them out by extending our arms to our sides, parallel to our shoulders, she would say, "Feel your integrity! Your shoulders speak to your integrity. Walk proudly in the world knowing you are an honorable person."

This lesson always stuck with me. When I found my shoulders slumping or hurting, I would remember Gloria's words and ask myself where I may not be living true to myself, disowning myself, or otherwise not being authentic in my life where I knew better, where I knew that I was somehow betraying some personal ethic. It was when I began to consider the intimate relationship I have with each part of my body; how each limb, each organ, and each muscle can speak to me, encouraging me to be honest about my emotional and spiritual health. In this way, my body slowly became a part of me which I could learn and gain greater knowledge about myself from. I moved from a place where, like many people, I had been raised to think of my body and all its desires as something to be controlled or overcome. This was a huge shift that started small. My body slowly began to mean more than the impression it made on other people or simply a vehicle to carry "the real me" around in. My body, and all its parts, was wise.

The nervous system is comprised of the brain and the spinal cord, and with the spinal cord itself being a symbol of our self, how we transform our being when looped with positive feedback and affirming self-talk that reinforces worthiness (Leo), indicates how intricately connected our self-concept and our conversations with ourselves are. The nervous system is complex, but basically it is the process with which information is communicated between different parts of the body, especially information about what different parts of your body are experiencing, and then communicates that back to your brain and sometimes, your awareness. From the emotions you feel physical discomfort or imbalances, even when they seem to be taking place in isolated regions of the body and send signals that set off activity in your brain. The nervous system is yet another powerful example of how we are self-contained yet multi-faceted, and how different segments, even those that seem unrelated, are actually an integral part of a whole.

The brain is responsible for, well, many things, but mainly it reflects, through activity, how we respond to the stimulation coming through our five senses. The brain controls our muscles and hormone levels, which are linked to what we feel, and being a part of the central nervous system, the brain and spinal cord play a symbolic role in how we perceive and communicate.

Gemini rules the shoulders and arms, the extensions of our body by which we share of ourselves and express our words. In fact, the hands, also under the rule of Gemini, are said to be used when talking, when this part of us is being accessed, creating a mental rhythm and beat to the words. This energy rules communication with others, especially in how we share our words in the moment. Our thought processes, the way we communicate with ourselves and perceive the world, is the other side of this duality. The way in which we talk to ourselves, and the spontaneity with which we allow our thoughts to come forth to our awareness, is what connects us to all the different stars and pockets of wisdom in the Universe, which is the essence of positive Gemini manifestation.

The main muscle of the shoulder is the deltoid, which gives the shoulder its round appearance. It consists of three heads. The posterior head forms the back of the deltoid muscle and contributes and supports a wide range of extensions. The anterior head comprises the front part of the muscle and work with the muscles in the chest in pressing actions. The lateral head on the side of the shoulder tucks into the arm and is involved in almost all shoulder movement.

The shoulder is comprised of three major bones, which meet at a joint in our skeletal structure. Joints speak to our ambition and destiny, and the wrist, elbow and shoulder contain joints that represent mobility, as we perceive what we need to communicate to achieve our goals (Capricorn). And as mentioned before, the shoulder symbolizes integrity, with the shoulder joints themselves symbolizing the connection between the consistency of our words and what we desire to do in the world.

The shoulder muscles are symbolic of the consistency between our thoughts and communications. The posterior deltoid represents the thoughts and perceptions that are not in our conscious awareness, but form the bulk of our understanding that guides our perceptions. The lateral head is symbolic of the integrity with which we trust our words and perceptions to guide us in navigating our immediate surroundings. The front head is symbolic of the integrity and consistency of our thought and communications, and how we believe we are perceived as a person of integrity, especially in conversation. Dumbbell raises are used to develop the front part of the shoulder. Lateral raises develop the lateral head, and the posterior head is strengthened with the bent fly.

70

The *bicep brachii* muscle consists of two heads, the long head and the short head. It lies in the upper arm. Its function is to aid in movement of the arm and to help flex and move the elbow and shoulder. Both heads start at the shoulder and tuck into the elbow region, with the short head creating the peak you see towards the middle and lower part of the flexed upper arm.

The biceps are the part of you that you flex when you tell someone you work out, to show and prove how strong you are. It is the bicep that captures the imagination, and it is the definitive symbol of an abundance of muscle. It is the part of communication that represents our actual communication ability with others, especially in words. This is where we show the strength of our mental communication skills by the way we use our words, understanding that words are power. The bicep symbolize how you give off yourself and show the world who you are through your words, at your very best. A good bicep exercise is a simple bicep curl.

The *triceps brachii* consists of three heads: lateral, long, and short. The triceps lies at the back of the arm. Sixty percent of the muscles in the upper arm are from the triceps. While the bicep helps your elbow bend, the triceps helps it to straighten. Triceps lie closer to the body and symbolize how we speak to ourselves. This is also an area that is often soft and requires deliberate effort to strengthen. This is how we talk to ourselves, how cohesive we are, how empowered, and if we perceive the world as orderly and intricately perfect. The triceps is a detailed muscle, with several distinctions, that express the intricacy with the way our thought processes and perceptions work. With the triceps, you give to yourself and pay attention to the thoughts that stream in your head. Considering that the triceps make up sixty percent of the muscle in your upper arm, the way you communicate with yourself is more significant than the strength you show others. An exercise for the triceps includes the triceps extension.

The forearm is comprised of several small muscles in the lower arm. The forearms are where we start to share off ourselves more spontaneously. It is the part of ourselves that we extend to and interact with the world, particularly through our words and communication. An exercise for the forearm is the reverse curl.

The hands, containing many small bones, provide details that allow us to grab hold of experiences. They symbolize our ability to grasp life firmly based on our mental understanding; the left hand represents grasping with an intuitive understanding, the right hand is symbolic of grasping life with action. The wrists provide a middle point, a place where our understanding meets our experience. Wrist curls with a lightweight exercise the wrist and hands.

To engage Gemini energy with yoga poses, try the Child Pose and Eagle Arms to connect with the shoulders and upper arms. To engage the entirety of the shoulders, arms, and wrists, try the Four Limbed Staff Pose, also called a Plank Pose.

Meditation for Gemini

Lie down or sit in a comfortable position. Close your eyes, or if you prefer, you can choose to start by softly gazing towards an image that feels calming to you. Start to pay attention to your breathing. Don't control it in any way yet, just pay attention to how you are breathing. Feel the breath move through your face, your nose, your mouth, fill your brain and move deeper into your body.

As you continue to breathe, begin to take your breath deeper. Take a few big breaths in. Feel the strength and power of your breath, filling you with energy and life. Feel your body rise and fall with each breath in. As your body relaxes more, you also can feel yourself more alert, as your mind fills with oxygen.

And as you continue to breathe, bring your attention to the exhale as well. Feel yourself releasing any thoughts of the past or the future. With each exhale, you release any feeling that is not part of this moment, right now. Observe the in and out of your breath. With each exhale you release, with each breath in, you feel more and more aware of this present moment. The present moment is truly all there is. The present moment is where the power is.

As you continue to breathe

Imagine the air around you as clear, light blue colored light. Notice the shading and beauty of this light. It feels calming and enlivening. It feels like an energy of love. This is the love of expression. It is the light of the love that reminds you that each moment, no matter how random it may seem on the surface, is an opportunity to share. To share is to love.

On each inhale, you are breathing in this brilliant pastel light.

Imagine this light flooding through your breath, into your nose, and moving through your throat, filling your body with this vibrant, blue energy.

Slowly become aware of how this breath is moving through your throat, your shoulders, down through your entire arms and into your fingers. This breath is alive, vibrating with love, infusing the top part of your body now.

Allow your mind to consider all things that this upper part of your body allows you to do. With your voice, you share the mind and the heart.

With your shoulders, you carry your self tall, and move through your world with grace and curiosity.

With your arms, you embrace life and embrace with love.

With your hands, you hold onto life. You grasp opportunities and connect ideas with new people.

And as you continue to breathe

Gently bring your attention back to your throat. Imagine a wheel, spinning the vibrant blue light you are breathing now. Imagine this spinning wheel of light clear your throat, releasing anything that gets in the way of your highest expression.

And as you continue to breathe...

And as you continue to place your attention on your throat.

There is a unique expression that you are here to share in this life and in this world.

A unique wisdom that desires to be known and said through you

With your attention on your throat, and bathed in the calming, beautiful blue light of your breath, ask yourself,

"What is it that I desire to say?"

"What is it that I have to express?"

Allow your answers to come forward naturally, in their own time.

Sit with your answers now.

Now gently bring your attention to your mantra for this meditation:

"I express myself authentically."

"There is always something new to discover."

"I have something unique to share."

Repeat these words to yourself. Feel these words merge with the bright, clear vibrant blue light, this energy of authentic expression, and the peace that it brings, flowing within you.

"I express myself authentically."

"There is always something new to discover."

"I have something unique to share."

As you continue to breathe

Feel yourself filled with gratitude, for whatever insight has presented itself to you. Whatever vision, whatever feeling. Affirm within you that there is wisdom in this exact moment.

Imagine yourself giving yourself a big hug. A burst of your own love. Knowing that as you continue to express yourself authentically, there will also be love available to you.

As you continue to breathe

Bring your attention gently to your breath. The feeling of your breath moving through your throat, your shoulders, your arms and your hands.

Give them thanks for all they are, all they have touched, felt, all they represent, and all they do.

As you continue to breathe

Bring your attention gently to your breath. The feeling of your breath moving through your nose, your face, and your mouth.

Gently, as you connect more strongly to breath, bring your attention to your five senses. Give them thanks for all they are, all they have seen, touched, smelled, tasted, and heard, and all they do.

As you continue to breathe

Gently feel yourself being in this present moment more and more. Begin to move your fingers and toes, with an awareness of the parts of your body in contact with a surface.

As you continue to breathe

Come back into this moment, and gently, as you are ready, open your eyes.

As you come back into this moment, and into your conscious awareness…

Jot down any thoughts that you'd like to affirm or remember in a notebook or recording device near you. And before you get up, be sure to thank this space that you were in, knowing that it was exactly as it needed to be.

Cancer

Home, Food, Spiritual, Emotional, and Physical Nurturance

Moon

Water Element

Pearl, Moonstone

Water Lilies, White Roses, Moonwort

Silver, Pearl White

"I Am at Home"

This is the sign that rules motherhood, mothers, home, and home-identity. There are powerful emotional turns associated with this part of us, but that is because the sign of Cancer is about learning the difference between emotional reactions that come from the past or intuitive insight. When channeled correctly, Cancer is a vibration that can be very healing through understanding where care needs to be given on a deep, emotional and intuitive level. However, improper channelling can make the Cancer vibration difficult because of the sheer force and power of emotion; emotional turns and yes, swings. Just as the mother will put on a brave face to protect her child's fragile life, Cancer is also symbolic of a tough exterior hiding deep sensitivity and bonds to the past. Strong Cancer placements in a chart would indicate a strong bond with the main maternal figure.

This is the part of us that is very interested in persona; building a shell. The lesson is to integrate the outer with the inner. The parts of the body associated with this segment of the cosmos are the breasts, stomach, the alimentary canal and the front part of the core. Its mantra is "I care for myself and others."

Our breasts tissue consists of mainly of fat, and for women the mammary glands, which carry milk for the purpose of nourishing one's own child. The breasts are most symbolic of feminine energy, particularly sacred feminine energy with its qualities of sensitivity and caring. The breasts are symbolic of our willingness or ability to care for and nurture others.

The female breasts in particular are associated with nurturance. Being willing to nurture is one of the greatest spiritual lessons, cultivated over a lifetime. Nurturing requires paying attention to our emotional needs, and this part of the body is powerfully associated with the segment of the cosmos that has to do with honoring what we really feel and being willing to learn from emotions. Experiencing tenderness of the breasts can be used as a reminder to listen and ask yourself "what can I do to nurture myself emotionally right now." The breasts are also symbolic of a heightened intuition, or intuition that is asking to be heard.

The stomach is an organ and part of the digestive system. After we chew our food, which breaks down our food initially, the stomach is the next place our nourishment goes so that it can be extracted of nutrients that will be absorbed into our blood stream and be used by our body. The stomach has four sections through which our food travels before entering the small intestines (Virgo) for further processing. The stomach is symbolic of our willingness or ability to receive love, and take the love we receive and integrate it deeply within us.

Plato believed that we each are comprised of three souls. The first soul is in our head, and is the higher part of us, connected to wisdom and rational thought. It is the immortal part of us. The second soul is in the thorax, and comprises our courage, passion, and other higher human qualities that are mortal, and will die with our body. Our third soul is found in the stomach, and is the passionate, lustful part of being human that we must contend with as part of being on earth. It contains the wisdom of understanding the benefits of learning from our feelings and passions. I am reminded of a friend who told me that every attraction and passion does not need to be followed, it just tells you that there is a lesson here and to pay attention. The stomach is therefore an area to pay attention to, for it reveals some of the key lessons, through its turbulence of feeling, that we are meant to learn at any given point in our lives, and should especially be listened to when there seems to be a lot of activity, and the feelings are coming on strong.

The alimentary canal is the entire pathway that food travels, from the moment it enters our mouth, to the time it leaves our body out the other end. The connection to the alimentary canal speaks to nourishment; from the moment we give something to ourselves, process it, and trust that we will release what we no longer need. Though the entire process of nourishment is indicated, it is what takes place in the stomach, the first and most central place that the digestive process takes place, that speaks to our willingness to be nourished. Problems with digestion, particularly that which takes place in the stomach, speaks to our central, most foundational feelings and beliefs about our worthiness to receive love, particularly our own love, in the form of care. Any unwillingness or discontent with the love we receive, and any mixed feelings, can manifest as discomfort here.

In addition, when the fear of being rejected is stronger than our desire to be true to ourselves, or when the fear that another may abandon us overtakes the knowledge that as long as you are there for yourself, as long as you do not abandon you, you will really be OK, these examples of misdirected sensitivity can express themselves as physical problems in these areas of the body.

Cancer rules the front part of the core, also known as the abdominals, which are comprised of four distinct muscle parts. The *rectus abdominus* are comprised of the upper abs. We feel those when we do a crunch and comprise the six-pack effect above and around the belly button that is visible on people who appear very fit. The lower abs continue the *rectus abdominus* below the belly button. These muscles cross each other in six groups that can be seen when this muscle is developed and grown.

The lower abs contain the *pyramidalis* muscle, which is triangular. The external and internal obliques run along the sides (ribs and pelvis) of and beneath the *rectus abdominus*. The *transverse abdominus* lies horizontally across the entire area. It has small sections that can be seen on the outer sides of the obliques when very well developed. The transverse makes the entire front part of the core strong and holds it together. This is the deepest muscle in the abs. It protects and supports the underlying organs and spine.

These are the parts of the body that we first connected to in our mother. It is our first, most immediate contact, and the first place of intimacy we know. As such, they become parts of ourselves that we are most intimate with.

Your core is your center, your foundation. It is the place you look and judge your own physicality. Most of the time, we keep this part of our body hidden, but when we reveal ourselves or evaluate ourselves, one tilt of the head down, a quick touch, and we connect to our own flesh. It is called the core for a reason. It is our past, and our home, especially that internal place of safety that is our inner home; that is the core of us. Everything else is built on top of the foundation of our past and our security. But the thing is, our past is up for interpretation- two people can go through similar childhood experiences but perceive them differently, and therefore have it influence them differently. Being able to interpret our past in a way that empowers us and grants us strength, and also provides us with an inner feeling of security, keeps our core strong. Knowing who we are and what we feel, outside of the influences and opinions of others, keeps us connected to our core.

Considering the fact that Cancer rules the front part of the core, it is the sense of self with which we approach the world; the aspects of self we are conscious of also speak to the future we are creating. Our stomach is also the one part of the body we might judge most, and look to determine our physical rightness. In this way, it is our own judgements of our stomach that can be the source of disempowerment. It is through acceptance and celebration that we come into our truth and the core of who we are. Our stomach is also the metaphorical place from which life rises, an indication of our ability to accept ourselves as magnificent creators. The stomach, when it holds generous size, has been linked to prosperity and fertility, as seen in the generous disposition of the Laughing Buddha, long held as symbolic of luck and success.

Honoring our feelings, and a commitment to feeling the strength of our core and the full sensitivity of our emotions, makes us surer of who we are. Once we are sure enough, we can stay centered in our newfound knowledge, and we can now approach the world from this place of assurance that comes from knowing and accepting ourself deeply. It is a strength that cannot be deterred by the opinions or perceptions of others.

Exercises include a simple crunch, and more precise or complex variations of it. Yoga poses include the Plank position, for its reliance on maintaining core form, and the Cat-Cow pose.

Meditation for Cancer

Lie down or sit in a comfortable position. Close your eyes, or if
you prefer, you can choose to start by softly gazing towards an
image that feels calming to you. Start to pay attention to your
breathing. Don't control it in any way yet, just pay attention to
how you are breathing. Feel the breath move through your face,
your nose, your mouth, fill your brain and move deeper into your
body.

As you continue to breathe, begin to take your breath deeper. Take a few big breaths in. Feel the strength and power of your breath, filling you with energy and life. Feel your body rise and fall with each breath in. As your body relaxes more, you also can feel yourself more alert, as your mind fills with oxygen.

And as you continue to breathe, bring your attention to the exhale as well. Feel yourself releasing any thoughts of the past or the future. With each exhale, you release any feeling that is not part of this moment, right now. Observe the in and out of your breath. With each exhale you release, with each breath in, you feel more and more aware of this present moment. The present moment is truly all there is. The present moment is where the power is.

As you continue to breathe

Imagine the air around you as a soothing, white, pearlescent colored light. Notice the shading and beauty of this pearlescent light. It feels calming and soothing. It feels like an energy of the love of home. It is here that you find yourself most comfortable, most at ease. It is here that you know you are among family, no matter where you go, or with whom you are.

Imagine this soothing white, pearlescent colored light move with your breath, down into your chest and into your stomach. Feel this light nourish your body and your soul. Imagine this light filled with nourishing pearls, each one with a concentrated dose of self love, self acceptance. As each pearl lights up within you, it fills you with a feeling of comfort. It fills you with a feeling of being truly comfortable within your own body and within your skin.

Sit with this light, filling you with love that allows you to feel more and more and at peace, more and more familiar, with the perfection of who you are, right now.

And as you continue to breathe the white, pearlescent colored light around you

Gently bring your attention to the parts of your body that are in contact with the surface beneath you. It might be though your legs resting on a chair, or touching the ground beneath you. Perhaps your feet are on the ground. Gently feel yourself connected to the surface of the Earth. Supported by the Earth. Know that this support is always there.

Now, imagine the roots of a tree growing out from the surfaces of your body, and reaching into the ground. These roots run deep, deep through the surface of the Earth, and deeper still, right to the core of the Earth. You become aware of the power and strength of these roots, fully grounding you, and connecting you

These roots speak to your connection to the physical plane. Your ancestors and the past they represent. You can see one of these roots light up with unconditional love and acceptance. It is inviting you to travel in its direction. See yourself traveling down, using this single root as a pathway, down through the path and towards a beautiful light.

As you move closer to this light, you can see a room. In this room, sits a person you have never seen before, but they feel familiar. They are glowing in love, with a look on their face and in their eyes of unconditional acceptance and pride for you.

Go to this person, and sit with them. This is one of your countless ancestors. They know your life, all your growth, your feelings, and every thing that has brought you to this moment, that has made you who you are today.

This person has a message, just for you. A message of love. A message of pride. A message of wisdom. Take this moment, and let them speak to you now. Take your time with this step, to receive the message they give.

As you continue to breathe the soothing, white, pearlescent colored air

Reach out to this person. Hold their hands, and together, gently bring your attention to your mantra for this meditation,

"I am at home."

"I am supported by the past and connected to my future."

"I am at comfortable in my body and I am at home with myself."

Feel these words merge with the light in the room, and the light within you. And gently repeat your affirmations now

"I am at home."

"I am supported by the past and connected to my future."

"I am at comfortable in my body and I am at home with myself."

As you continue to breathe the soothing, white, pearlescent colored air

Feel yourself filled with gratitude, for this moment with your ancestor, for the sacrifices and love they gave that have been a part of your journey, bringing you to this present day. Whatever insight has presented itself to you through them, whatever vision, whatever feeling, feel gratitude for all of it. Affirm within you that there is wisdom in this exact moment.

Give your ancestor a big hug, filled with love and gratitude. Know that this person is always there, always a part of you.

As you continue to breathe

See yourself get up and begin to step away, gently at first. You are moving away, but you continue to feel the connection and the gratitude move through you. Continue to feel yourself walk back through this root pathway that brought you here. Slowly walking this path up, from this room in the core of the earth, up through the layers of this planet, and back towards your awareness of your own body and your breath

As you continue to breathe

Bring your attention gently to your breath. The feeling of your breath moving through your nose, your face, and your mouth.

As you continue to breathe

Gently feel yourself being in this present moment more and more. Begin to move your fingers and toes, with an awareness of the parts of your body in contact with a surface.

As you continue to breathe

Come back into this moment, and gently, as you are ready, open your eyes.

As you come back into this moment, and into your conscious awareness…

Jot down any thoughts that you'd like to affirm or remember in a notebook or recording device near you. And before you get up, be sure to thank this space that you were in, knowing that it was exactly as it needed to be.

Leo

Personal Power, Ego, Performance

Sun

Fire Element

Amber, Sunstone

Sunflowers, Marigold

Gold, Orange, Yellow

"I Am Worthy of Shining"

This is the part of the cosmos that rules pleasure and leisure. Leo rules the heart metaphorically. There is a fire, or light, in the heart that desires to be shared and recognized. It is undeniable in its presence, and so is Leo energy! This is the sign of confidence, charisma, and dramatics. Leo energy is creative. It is a trust in your own creativity and the belief that you have something special that deserves to be shared and seen. This takes confidence to the next level. With Aries, the first archetype reflected in the cosmos that is associated with fire, it was more about proving that you can excel. With Leo, it is about believing that you, as an independent creative source, deserve not only to excel, but also express and shine. This is the sign of fun. This is the sign of royalty and entitlement. An imbalance of this energy occurs when we feel like something about us is just "one of the herd," or similar to someone else, because it is uniqueness and specialness that desires to be recognized. That is when the energy gets stuck. The parts of the body this part of the cosmos corresponds to are the heart, the upper back, the chest muscles, and the spinal cord. The mantra for Leo is "I am the greatest."

This is the part of the sky that rules royalty and also ego. In Freudian psychology terminology, the ego is the part of the psyche that harmonizes between our instinctual passionate desires, which forms a middle ground between two other parts of our psyche, the Id, which forms our most passionate desires and urges, and our conscious, also called our Super-ego, which is the perfect concept in our minds of who we think we should be. The

Ego finds a balance between ourselves that we judge imperfect, and our most perfect selves.

The Latin translation of ego is "I, myself," and when we speak of ego in a new age or self-help sense, it tends to denote an exaggerated self-importance. The ego itself does not need to be thought of this way. A balanced ego allows us the feeling of worthiness, required to care for ourselves, believing we are entitled to the best health today and also an appearance we can be proud of. However, ego and entitlement, carried too far, can lead us to take actions to demonstrate our superiority over others. This is an imbalance of this part of us, one done to mask feelings of inferiority.

The heart is a vital organ that is made out of a type of muscle unique to itself. This type of muscle, known as cardiac muscle, does not get tired or strained nearly as quickly as our other muscles so. The purpose of the heart is to circulate oxygen throughout our body. It does this by taking deoxygenated blood into the right side of the heart, moving that blood through the lungs, where it receives oxygen, and then into the left side of the heart. From there, the blood is pumped back into the body. The beating we feel and hear in our heart is due to the force of this pumping action. With every rhythmic beat, we are replenished.

The heart muscle is the most central organ in the body and most powerfully symbolizes love and sharing. It is love that affirms our worthiness to give to ourselves, and also love that asserts we are worthy of sharing. This part of the body asserts a sense of self that is all our own, self-conceptualized and distinct. It serves as a symbol of our importance by doing all that work only to give to ourself, while recognizing that everyone has a heart. This is also a symbol of replenishment and revitalizations, indicating that our self-concept and ability to love is always able to take in new information and share in new, renewed, and more authentic ways. Plato considered the heart the place where our lustful drives meet our rationality, and it was in the heart where, much like Freud's concept of the ego, we made a balanced decision that affirmed who we are, when we are at the best that we can be for today.

The major muscle in the chest region is the *pectoralis major*, also called the pectorals, or simply the pecs, which lies closest to the skin, and just under the fatty breast tissue. Shaped like a fan, the muscle extends from under the arms to the center of the chest in two sections, going as far down to the ribs and as high as the clavicle near the shoulder.

The *pectoralis minor* lies underneath the *pectoralis major*. It is shaped like a triangle. The muscle starts at the ribs at its wider side and ends by tucking in just under the shoulder at its narrow side. It supports the separation between these two muscle groups.

If you think about the chest muscles, they have a wide range of cover that protects the heart muscle within. There are several striations to the pectorals that are visible when this area is well developed. The chest muscles speak to how willing you are to love yourself and others. The more the muscle lies near the center of your body, for example, the inner part of the *pectoralis major* muscles, or away from the surface, as is the case with *the pectoralis minor*, the more it is about the love you give yourself and the self-loving concept that you may have, or need to develop. The further into the muscle we go, the more it becomes about what love we are willing to share. The *pectoralis minor* in particular, builds a bridge from the scapula down to your ribs and thoracic wall. This path begins with your integrity (as connected with the way you communicate-Gemini), and draws inward on a slope that stabilizes the worthiness with which you hold yourself. It symbolizes how you use your words and perceptions to assert your sense of yourself. A strong *pectoralis minor* supports a balanced, affirming self-concept. The *pectoralis major*, and particularly the outer striations, are connected to the belief we have about sharing and showing love, and our willingness to demonstrate it.

Exercises that work this part of the body include chest exercises like push-ups, chest presses, and chest flys. The back is worked mainly through pull-ups, by extending and building the wide upper V shape of a well-developed back. You may be inspired to develop the inner pectoral muscles when learning to love yourself more deeply. This part of the body speaks to confidence, worthiness, and expanding one's creative ability.

The *trapezius* muscle lies in the center of your upper back, over the heart. It is diamond-shaped with the top point beginning at the base of the head, extending across and down towards the shoulders. It then extends down and ends in its other point in the center of your back. It works with your shoulders by connecting them to the back, allowing for greater movement and support. It is on our back, behind us, suggesting that our past experiences are central to our self-concept. The connection to the shoulders suggests that our previous experiences, which inform our self-concept, can support and enhance the integrity of our words.

All words hold integrity. The integrity of authentically aligning and revealing our self-concept comes forth in the things we say, sometimes in the most unconscious, casual things, or perhaps especially in those moments it is that we reveal who we really are and what we really believe about ourselves. Our deepest beliefs about our worthiness are revealed in our perceptions and communications. While the word integrity has been associated with morality, I would like to think of it more as consistency. Regardless of how thick our persona may be, a moment of reflection on our inner voice makes it clear how much we really value ourselves.

The *trapezius* muscles symbolize the support and the value we place on being consistent with a strong, loving self-concept and expressing that in the world. As a muscle it speaks to having a strong enough sense of self that you so share and are willing to interact in order to affirm a more loving self-concept. A simple exercise to work the *trapezius* is the shoulder shrug, holding two dumbbells in your hands, limp at your sides, and shrugging your shoulders.

The spinal cord is a part of the central nervous system, and works with the brain and nervous system, symbolic of communication, perception, and sharing (Gemini). The spinal cord runs along the back and is comprised of tissues and cells. It essentially sends signals from the brain out to the various parts of the body. It is the pathway that forms part of what we call the core, and that is appropriate considering that the sense of self and our belief in our worthiness forms part of a central understanding about who we are.

The spinal cord is also ruled by Leo, as is the *trapezius*, the large muscle that lies in the top part of the back and is intimately connected to the muscles of the shoulder. Again, we see how our communication and perception is interlinked to our ability to love. It is as if all the love we feel and have to share must be filtered through the perceptions and words we use if they are to know their full power.

Any heart strengthening cardio exercise with bring attention to this area. Yoga poses include the Camel Pose and Cobra Pose, for their ability to stretch the chest muscles. The Lion Pose is also helpful in engaging the lioness nature of the energy.

Meditation for Leo

Lie down or sit in a comfortable position. Close your eyes, or if you prefer, you can choose to start by softly gazing towards an image that feels calming to you. Start to pay attention to your breathing. Don't control it in any way yet, just pay attention to how you are breathing. Feel the breath move through your face, your nose, your mouth, fill your brain and move deeper into your body.

As you continue to breathe, begin to take your breath deeper. Take a few big breaths in. Feel the strength and power of your breath, filling you with energy and life. Feel your body rise and fall with each breath in. As your body relaxes more, you also can feel yourself more alert, as your mind fills with oxygen.

And as you continue to breathe, bring your attention to the exhale as well. Feel yourself releasing any thoughts of the past or the future. With each exhale, you release any feeling that is not part of this moment, right now. Observe the in and out of your breath. With each exhale you release, with each breath in, you feel more and more aware of this present moment. The present moment is truly all there is. The present moment is where the power is.

As you continue to breathe

Imagine the air around you as a bright, vibrant, gold colored light Notice the shading and beauty of this light. It feels calming and strengthening. It feels like an energy of love. This is the love of courage. It is the light of the love that reminds you that each moment where you are willing to live and willing to love is an act of courage.

On each inhale, you are breathing in this brilliant, vibrant gold light.

Imagine this light flooding through your breath, into your heart, and from your heart, radiating forward and filling your body with this vibrant, gold energy.

Slowly become aware of how this breath is moving into and through your heart. With each rise and fall of your breath, you can feel your heart intimately involved in the process.

And as you continue to breathe

Slowly, bring your attention to the beating of your heart. Notice its rhythm, bringing music into your body. Notice how your breath works with this beat of your heart, creating a song.

This song has a structure, and beat and a rhyme, just as your life has a rhythm, a purpose, and a meaning, even when it isn't apparent.

And as you continue to breathe

Gently bring your attention back to your heart. Imagine a wheel, spinning the vibrant gold light you are breathing now. Imagine this spinning wheel of light clear your heart, releasing anything that gets in the way of you sharing your heart purely and completely.

As you continue to breathe

Imagine your heart in your mind's eye. See it in front of you. What does it look like? How do you feel in its presence?

Now imagine yourself beginning to dialogue with your heart. Be willing to engage it in conversation.

With your attention on your heart, and bathed in the calming, beautiful gold light of breath, ask yourself:

"What does my heart desire?"

"What does my heart lead me towards?"

"What does my heart want me to know?"

Allow your answers to come forward naturally, in their own time.

Sit with your answers now.

Now gently bring your attention to your mantra for this meditation:

"I am worthy of shining."

"I am worthy of being seen."

"My heart is alive with courage and strength."

Repeat these words to yourself. Feel these words merge with the bright, clear vibrant gold light, this energy of love, passion, courage, and the peace that it brings, flowing within you.

"I am worthy of shining."

"I am worthy of being seen."

"My heart is alive with courage and strength."

As you continue to breathe

Feel yourself filled with gratitude, for whatever insight has presented itself to you. Whatever vision, whatever feeling. Affirm within you that there is wisdom in this exact moment.

Imagine yourself giving your heart a big hug. A burst of your own love. Knowing that as you continue to listen to your heart, there will also be love available to you.

As you continue to breathe

Bring your attention gently to your breath. The feeling of your breath moving through your heart, radiating forward from your chest.

As you continue to breathe

Bring your attention gently to your breath. The feeling of your breath moving through your nose, your face, and your mouth.

Gently feel yourself being in this present moment more and more. Begin to move your fingers and toes, with an awareness of the parts of your body in contact with a surface.

As you continue to breathe

Come back into this moment, and gently, as you are ready, open your eyes.

As you come back into this moment, and into your conscious awareness…

Jot down any thoughts that you'd like to affirm or remember in a notebook or recording device near you. And before you get up, be sure to thank this space that you were in, knowing that it was exactly as it needed to be.

Virgo

Service to Others, Expertise, Practice

Mercury, Night

Earth Element

Diamond, Jade, Jasper

Rosemary, Cornflower

Pastel Colors, Peach

"I Have Something to Give"

This part of the cosmos has a strong sense of self, of physical place, especially in the body. There is a very earthy beauty inherent in this sign, as it can feel the slightest difference in the body, and you can tell that when this energy is channeled in its higher understanding, it is very present in the moment. This is also the part of the sky that is concerned with orderly thoughts and ascribing the appropriate place for everything on a mental level. There is a strong work ethic and an understanding that the day, or the journey, is more important than the goal. This is the part of us that values independence as an important virtue, especially independence of thought. This is also the part of us that desires and works towards mastery, whether that is mastery over the self in terms of habits, or of a craft.

Virgo is the part of the sky that has to do with being of service and living a life that feels meaningful in the moment. It is one thing to reach for a goal (Capricorn), or to have an inspired vision (Sagittarius), but this is the practical business of living in a manner filled with practices and habits that feel like they are making some contribution, or otherwise part of a meaningful existence.

The flip side to the highly analyzing nature of this archetype within us is that if it is not channeled correctly, it results in highly neurotic and somewhat obsessive mental patterns. The solution is to live and put effort into daily practice that channel that energy towards artisanship, expertise, and mastery. Virgo corresponds to the kidneys, intestines, spleen, and lower digestive system parts of our body. Its mantra is: "Service is accomplishment."

The intestines are the final place that food goes to be squeezed of all its nutritive value that our body uses as part of meeting its needs or nourishment. This is the lower digestive system, the ability to be nourished even more deeply, being more discerning about what we will need to take the best of care for ourselves. Of the intestines, Plato thought that it was here that, because of our bowel movements, we are prevented from having an insatiable appetite, and thus living in gluttony, which is the enemy to philosophy and music. He thought that by its nature, the quality of gluttony was rebellious to our most divine self. The intestines thus represent the gift of slowing us down so that we are not consumed by a constant desire to feed an inner hunger. The intestines also make sure that whatever we do use to nourish ourself is fully utilized to our advantage, and satiates and satisfies to the best of its ability. This part of the sky is deeply connected with the body and preventative health practices, especially those that are practiced daily. By listening to our body and fully giving it what it needs, we satisfy urges that can free us to incorporate deeper understandings into our life. The Virgo archetype suggests that too much focus on the day can deprive us of the vision and detachment that is required in philosophical pursuit, and that a balance is needed of all archetypal energies if we are to cultivate an appreciation of the positives of the day, and also the ideas and inspiration that make life meaningful. Again, any energy carried too far goes out of balance.

The spleen is instrumental in our body's ability to regulate our red blood cell count, particularly in the event of circulatory shock.

The spleen also regulates iron, an essential mineral that gives life to our red blood cells. Iron is an element that is sacred to the mythological god Ares, and is symbolic of that archetypal energy as a part of our life force. Considering these connections between iron regulation, the spleen, and the Virgo archetype, it is a connection that we feel with this sacred energy in our bodies and in our daily practices that becomes symbolized here. It is powerful to consider how this Ares archetype part of us needs to be channeled into our daily lives, and a connection continuously sought, in order to keep the conversation we have with the spirit infused with body.

Plato considered the spleen to be the organ that keeps the liver functioning properly, or to put it more accurately, the liver (Sagittarius), which is associated with divination, uses the spleen. The spleen works to keep the liver clean and magnetizes any impurities towards itself so that the messages that do come through the liver are accurate and properly filtered. The connection that he draws between how the Virgo part of us is responsible for the Sagittarius part, and how the spleen, through its attention to the impurities, allows the enthused and faithful part of us (Sagittarius) to appropriately shine, suggests that the details of cleanliness on every level has to be attended to if our faith and optimism is to be genuine.

Exercises for this part of the body include leg raises with or without weights. Yoga poses include the Boat Pose and Cobra Pose, when focused on stretching right into the lower stomach.

Meditation for Virgo

Lie down or sit in a comfortable position. Close your eyes, or if you prefer, you can choose to start by softly gazing towards an image that feels calming to you. Start to pay attention to your breathing. Don't control it in any way yet, just pay attention to how you are breathing. Feel the breath move through your face, your nose, your mouth, fill your brain and move deeper into your body.

As you continue to breathe, begin to take your breath deeper. Take a few big breaths in. Feel the strength and power of your breath, filling you with energy and life. Feel your body rise and fall with each breath in. As your body relaxes more, you also can feel yourself more alert, as your mind fills with oxygen.

And as you continue to breathe, bring your attention to the exhale as well. Feel yourself releasing any thoughts of the past or the future. With each exhale, you release any feeling that is not part of this moment, right now. Observe the in and out of your breath. With each exhale you release, with each breath in, you feel more and more aware of this present moment. The present moment is truly all there is. The present moment is where the power is.

As you continue to breathe…

Imagine the air around you as a pure, pastel, peach colored light. Notice the shading and beauty of this light. It feels calming and strengthening. It feels like an energy of love. This is the love of service. It is the light of the love that reminds you that each moment where you are willing to be truly present, is an act of service to others, to yourself, and to us all.

On each inhale, you are breathing in this pure, pastel, peach, vibrant light.

Imagine this light flooding through your breath, into your body, right into your lower stomach, radiating and nourishing your body, filling your body with this vibrant peach energy.

Slowly become aware of how this breath is moving into and through your digestive track. From your throat, down through your stomach, and into your intestines. With each rise and fall of your breath, you can feel each breath move into your lower stomach and nourish every cell in your entire body through the digestive process.

And as you continue to breathe

Slowly, bring your attention to the lower half of your stomach. Notice each second of the process, paying attention to the minutia of movement in your lower stomach.

And as you continue to breathe

Imagine a wheel at the center of your lower stomach, spinning the vibrant, peach-colored light you are breathing now. Imagine this spinning wheel of light in this part of your body, releasing any emotion you no longer need, that might be associated here. Give this part of your body your full love and acceptance.

As you continue to breathe

Imagine yourself in your mind's eye, as you are right now, in meditation. It is as if you are sitting in the same room, observing yourself. See yourself with eyes of love and acceptance. Release any judgement. See all of you as perfect, exactly as you are right now.

This person, in front of you, has something to give. This person is here to serve, to be useful, to give your love and your time to something that matters to you. And if it matters to you, it matters.

Connect with the feeling of love, moving through you. See it as the vibrant, peach-colored light around you now

Affirm to yourself now:

"I have something to give"

"I am perfect, exactly as I am right now"

"Every moment, no matter how small or how big, holds the sacred."

Gently notice any resistance that might arise, see it for what it is, not arising from love, and let it go. Just put it to the side for now, and gently bring yourself back to your affirmations. Repeat these words to yourself. Feel these words merge with the vibrant, peach-colored light around you now, flowing within you.

"I have something to give"

"I am perfect, exactly as I am right now"

"There is perfection in this moment"

As you continue to breathe

Feel yourself filled with gratitude, for whatever insight has presented itself to you. Whatever vision, whatever feeling. Affirm within you that there is wisdom in this exact moment.

As you continue to breathe

Bring your attention gently to your breath. The feeling of your breath moving through your nose, your face, and your mouth.

As you continue to breathe

Gently feel yourself being in this present moment more and more. Begin to move your fingers and toes, with an awareness of the parts of your body in contact with a surface.

As you continue to breathe

Come back into this moment, and gently, as you are ready, open your eyes.

As you come back into this moment, and into your conscious awareness...

Jot down any thoughts that you'd like to affirm or remember in a notebook or recording device near you. And before you get up, be sure to thank this space that you were in, knowing that it was exactly as it needed to be.

Libra

Symmetry, Higher Beauty, Architecture, Partnerships

Venus, Night

Air Element

Lapis Lazuli, Sapphire

Violets, White Roses

Royal Blue, Amethyst

"I See the Beauty in All Things"

The part of the cosmos that addresses democracy, fairness, considering all perspectives, and relating to people, especially through communication, and relationships. This is the part of us that cares about beautiful ideas and ideals of symmetry. There is a strong need for harmony with the Libra vibration, and the parts of the body associated with Libra correlates to being in a harmonic state in specific areas of our lives and make us feel like we are on an equilibrium. The differing opinions of others are not taken personally, though there is the desire to reach commonality and compromise, as a way of learning about ourselves.

It is the sign of relationships and relating, or seeing and learning about yourself as reflected in the eyes of another. It is also the sign of the higher concepts of beauty and truth, and ethics. The mantra is "I have to know you to know my truth." Moderation in all things is essential. This part of the cosmos is symbolized in the lumbar region (lower back), buttocks, and skin.

The muscles that correspond with this part of the cosmos are the *latissimus dorsi*, also called the lats. It extends from the shoulder blades down through the lumbar region, and is connected by some of its upper layers with the *trapezius* muscle (Leo). In its deepest layers, the *latissimus* connects with the pectoral muscles (Leo), the biceps (Gemini) and obliques (Cancer). It symbolizes how the way we relate to people on a personal level, especially in romantic relationships, is intimately connected to our past, our self-concept, and our communication and perception style. Some of the best exercises to strengthen this area of the body include pull-ups for the upper part of the lumbar, and rows for the sides.

Your lower lumbar and back region forms the back portion of what is called the "core." This is a part of your center, and the part that supports you the most. In fact, it seems that all movement of the body comes from this place. Libra is the sign of relating and relationships; it is seeing yourself in the mirror of another person, considering the world and you from their perspective. The relationships we have, when utilized for the lessons they hold, return us to ourselves. Our relationships define our backbone. Our experiences in love define us. They lend to the most powerful human experiences that lead to choices that define us, in some cases, forever.

The glutes, also called the buttocks, are comprised of three main muscles. The *gluteus maximus* is the main muscle in your buttocks and allows the area to appear round and protrude. Its function in our body is to help us stand. The *gluteus medius* is on the outer side of your buttocks. The *gluteus minimus* lies deep behind the maximus and minimus. The medius and minimus lets you move your leg in and out and stand on one leg.

Just as the buttocks are the seat when we sit, it is also symbolic of our own understanding of our personal seat of power. Working the glute muscles might inspire a feeling of returning to one's power, for bringing in an awareness of where someone else ends and where you begin. Power is a fascinating and intricate thing.

Emotions, especially those that come up in feelings of partnership, are particularly a way of wielding power because they make us feel vulnerable.

One of the best glute exercises is the squat. Through utilizing variations, you can feel exactly which angles of the glutes are being worked, depending on where you feel you need the stimulation. Doing squats builds the *gluteus maximus*, making the shape of that area more defined, but be very careful to maintain proper form throughout the exercise. Other great glute exercises are hip extensions and hip abductions, performed on all fours or standing, moving from front to back or laterally out to the side. The lateral hip abductions, especially standing, engage the medius and minimus with a greater intensity.

Our skin is the largest organ on our body. It has many layers that protect the inner contents, but also can reveal what is inside. Glowing skin is said to represent a person who is happy and healthy. My skin can appear differently depending on how well I am taking care of myself physically and emotionally. The skin also helps absorb stimulus from the sun and convert it into vitamin D that is then integrated into our entire system. In our kidneys, vitamin D is then converted by our body into a hormone that allows us to absorb calcium. Our skin is all-encompassing, and is symbolic of how we feel about our worthiness to relate closely with another person, one-on-one.

As we get older, we may find our skin relax, just as we relax more fully into ourselves. As we become more at ease and more comfortable with our skin, so too may our skin represent a more comfortable state of being.

Our kidneys are deeply connected to purification in that they produce urine that allows us to release toxins. The kidneys also regulate our blood pressure and electrolytes. The kidneys are symbolic of equilibrium and balance in body and thought. This is the part of our body that speaks to our ability and willingness to compromise in ways that will either affirm our equilibrium or throw us off balance.

The Libra energy is often associated with our one on one relationships. Partnerships of all kinds correspond to this energy. Any relationships involves some give and some take. It is a constant act of finding balance between two people, who might have very different motivations or core desires. It is in relating to another that we are invited to see ourselves in new ways, to discover who we are. An expanded view of ourselves is not found in taking another's opinion as our own. Rather, it is found in paying attention to our own responses, and the emotional skills we are asked to cultivate through our interactions with them. In this way, it is through partnership that we are invited to see ourselves differently, to see ourselves anew, as reflected in the eyes of another.

Yoga poses for this part of the body include the Cat Pose, and the Downward Dog.

Meditation for Libra

Lie down or sit in a comfortable position. Close your eyes, or if you prefer, you can choose to start by softly gazing towards an image that feels calming to you. Start to pay attention to your breathing. Don't control it in any way yet, just pay attention to how you are breathing. Feel the breath move through your face, your nose, your mouth, fill your brain and move deeper into your body.

As you continue to breathe, begin to take your breath deeper. Take a few big breaths in. Feel the strength and power of your breath, filling you with energy and life. Feel your body rise and fall with each breath in. As your body relaxes more, you also can feel yourself more alert, as your mind fills with oxygen.

And as you continue to breathe, bring your attention to the exhale as well. Feel yourself releasing any thoughts of the past or the future. With each exhale, you release any feeling that is not part of this moment, right now. Observe the in and out of your breath. With each exhale you release, with each breath in, you feel more and more aware of this present moment. The present moment is truly all there is. The present moment is where the power is.

As you continue to breathe

Imagine the air around you as a pure, pastel, baby-blue colored light. Notice the shading and beauty of this light. It feels calming and balancing. It feels like an energy of love. This is the love of harmony. It is the light of the love that reminds you that the middle way is the way of peace and the way of power. Each moment where you are willing to bring balance, is an act of beauty to others, to yourself, and to us all.

On each inhale, you are breathing in this pure, pastel baby-blue, vibrant light.

Imagine this light flooding through your breath, into your body, right into your kidneys, radiating and nourishing your body, filling your body with this vibrant baby-blue energy.

Become aware of how this breath is moving into and through your skin, radiating forward. See yourself now, glowing from this calming, healing, vibrant blue light, from the inside out. With each rise and fall of your breath, you can feel each breath move into your kidneys, through your body, and outwards forward through your skin, filling your aura. This beautiful baby-blue light is nourishing each of the cells of your entire body, and bringing you calm, ease, balance, and harmony.

And as you continue to breathe

Imagine yourself sitting, perhaps it's on the floor with your legs crossed, or perhaps in a chair. You are sitting in front of you, as if you were looking in a mirror, but it's real. You are facing yourself, looking yourself in the eyes.

See yourself with eyes of love. Who you are looking at, you have love for. What you are seeing as you look at yourself, you love what you see. Take notice of the physical features you love about yourself. Contemplate their significance to you that makes them that much more beautiful. Perhaps you like the shape, perhaps it is like a family member you loved, or perhaps it is a part of you that has helped you have an experience that was meaningful to you. That time you saw something beautiful with your eyes, or felt something lovely on your skin. This is you, and your experience is beautiful in its entirety.

And as you continue to breathe

Take your perception of yourself deeper. Look at the inner qualities you hold. The things you love about yourself. The qualities of character, of resolve, kindness, and of perspective. Spend some time now contemplating the inner attributes of you that make you beautiful.

As you continue to breathe

Now imagine that these two versions of yourself both want something that feels at odds with each other. It could be something superficial. The time you didn't know if you should choose instant gratification or the long term goal. The time you saw how two sets of circumstances could make you happy, so you didn't know what to choose. Now see yourself holding your own hands and finding peace with this situation. You will choose the middle way, together. Find the path of moderation, together.

As you continue to breathe

See yourself fill with love for this person, for yourself, knowing that this is an amazing partnership you will continue to cultivate for the rest of your life. Feel this love flow through both versions of yourself.

As you continue to breathe

Affirm to yourself now:

"I see the beauty in all things"

"I see beauty in myself, exactly as I am right now"

"I see beauty in my path, exactly as I am right now"

Gently notice any resistance that might arise, see it for what it is, not arising from love, and let it go. Just put it to the side for now, and gently bring yourself back to your affirmations.

"I see the beauty in all things"

"I see beauty in myself, exactly as I am right now"

"I see beauty in my path, exactly as I am right now"

Feel these words merge with the bright, vibrant, pastel baby-blue light, this energy of love, balance, harmony, and the peace that it brings, flowing within you and flowing through you.

As you continue to breathe

Feel yourself filled with gratitude, for whatever insight has presented itself to you. Whatever vision, whatever feeling. Affirm within you that there is wisdom in this exact moment.

As you continue to breathe

Bring your attention gently to your breath. The feeling of your breath moving through your body, radiating forward from within, through your skin, and throughout your aura.

As you continue to breathe

Bring your attention gently to your breath. The feeling of your breath moving through your nose, your face, and your mouth.

As you continue to breathe

Gently feel yourself being in this present moment more and more. Begin to move your fingers and toes, with an awareness of the parts of your body in contact with a surface.

As you continue to breathe

Come back into this moment, and gently, as you are ready, open your eyes.

As you come back into this moment, and into your conscious awareness...

Jot down any thoughts that you'd like to affirm or remember in a notebook or recording device near you. And before you get up, be sure to thank this space that you were in, knowing that it was exactly as it needed to be.

Scorpio

Solving Mysteries, Wealth, Rebirth, Truth, Transformation

Mars Night, Pluto

Water Element

Garnet, Carnelian

Chrysanthemum, Dragons Blood

Dark Purple, Black, Grey

"I Know My Truth"

Scorpio is the part of the cosmos that speaks to our deeper occult perception and our ability to manipulate energy. The most significant visual that encapsulates what this energy is about understands Scorpio as Fixed Water, which brings up the image of a well or other undisturbed body of water. It seems so still on the surface, but you can sense that it actually runs very deep and there is a whole lot just under the surface that you cannot see and may never get to see. What happens to water when it is fixed, like in a well, unmoved, and unaffected by winds or tides? It stagnates and can become a breeding ground for insects and other festering life forms that can take over the health of that water. The water needs to actively be engaged so that it can move. Movement needs to happen, sweat must occur to get the impurities out, so that the water of the body can stay fresh.

When conscious of this energy, it can represent the psyche that runs so deep, but if worked on, can go through a total transformation. However, if the psyche is not worked on, then we can play power games with others and ourselves. With our Scorpio energy, we can achieve great things because of the sheer force of emotional will. This is survivor energy, and when people are acting from the higher vibration of this, they can see or feel, the truth to any situation. This is the part of us that desires to merge and share, and that includes intimately.

This archetype of the sky connects to the reproductive system, sexual organs, bowels, and excretory system.

Scorpio has a reputation of governing sex. This is also the place where transformation happens. Scorpio is very important energy to cultivate when undertaking weight loss as a spiritual pursuit, because one of the myths associated with Scorpio is the snake and the life, death and rebirth cycle it represents as it sheds its dead skin many times, a physical representation of the Sufi saying (and also its mantra): "die a thousand times before you die."

Our bowels allow us to release the dead byproduct of the food we ate, having extracted all of its nutritional value. Here we let go of what we no longer need in a manner that is deemed disgusting, shameful, or most private. Interestingly, our sexual organs and processes, for much of cultural history, have been described using the same words.

To know and trust another deeply is to give away a part of us. No matter how much we tell ourselves that sex is for sport, there is trust involved. There is a part of us that we must give away, let die, if we are to be transformed by the experience.

Our reproductive system, symbolic of merging to the point of rebirth, is a largely hidden process that happens in private, a clandestine process within. This part of the body is symbolic of creation, and our creative energy. How we direct this energy towards the manifestation of our creative projects will be reflected here.

Scorpio rules the parts of the body that pertain to merging with another in the most intimate moments, and also the places of our body from which we release all those rejected things, sometimes in a manner most undeniable.

The excretory system is responsible for eliminating waste, ridding our bodies of waste via our breath and pores, It is here that sweat as a purifier falls under. Under Taurus, we are adding things to our lives and ourselves, those things that we think we need, that bring us a sense of self and pleasure. In its polar sign, Scorpio, we get rid of what we do not need in favor of something more meaningful and authentic. To not allow ourselves to rid us of the things that we do not need leads to hanging on to that what is ultimately harmful. Holding on leads to a poisonous internal environment. This is true of emotions, spirit, and reflects in our body.

This is also the part of the sky that rules not only life and rebirth, but also death. In many ways, this whole book is an exploration of the two sides of Ares, and Scorpio represents and reflects its night aspect, its shade, that goes beyond action and turns inward, introspective. The introspection is needed, for it is in the period just before the rebirth can happen that we have to identify what needs to die. This is why Scorpio also rules psychoanalysis. Just like our body may go through shedding, which leads to a transformation; if it is to last, it has to be holistic. It has to incorporate psychological understanding of what is being held onto, so that it can be focused on, and eventually all that work is done so that it can be released. Those secrets (this is the sector of the sky ruling secrets that we do not want told to anyone), become known. They remind us that we are only as sick as the secrets we keep. We share them with one other truly trusted person. The secrets of our psyche and the secrets of our body, in moments of deep intimacy. In this process, we give away something of our selves. We die willingly so that we can be renewed and reborn.

Yoga poses include the One Legged King Pigeon Pose, and the Tree Pose.

Meditation for Scorpio

Lie down or sit in a comfortable position. Close your eyes, or if you prefer, you can choose to start by softly gazing towards an image that feels calming to you. Start to pay attention to your breathing. Don't control it in any way yet, just pay attention to how you are breathing. Feel the breath move through your face, your nose, your mouth, fill your brain and move deeper into your body.

As you continue to breathe, begin to take your breath deeper. Take a few big breaths in. Feel the strength and power of your breath, filling you with energy and life. Feel your body rise and fall with each breath in. As your body relaxes more, you also can feel yourself more alert, as your mind fills with oxygen.

And as you continue to breathe, bring your attention to the exhale as well. Feel yourself releasing any thoughts of the past or the future. With each exhale, you release any feeling that is not part of this moment, right now. Observe the in and out of your breath. With each exhale you release, with each breath in, you feel more and more aware of this present moment. The present moment is truly all there is. The present moment is where the power is.

As you continue to breathe…

Imagine the air around you as a pure, vibrant, purple colored light. Notice the shading and beauty of this light. It feels protective and honest. It feels like an energy of power. This is the love of transformation and healthy change. It is the light of this love that reminds you that life is in constant flux, and it is in staying honest with ourselves, that we find our way towards personal power. Each moment where you are willing to be honest, it is an act of transformation, for yourself, and for us all.

On each inhale, you are breathing in this pure, vibrant, purple-colored light.

Imagine this light flooding through your breath, first into your psyche, and then down into your reproductive organs, and through your entire body. Radiating health and nourishing your body. Filling you with this vibrant, pure, purple-colored energy.

Become aware of the flow of this breath circulating through your body. See yourself now, glowing from this protective, focused, honest, vibrant purple light, from the inside out. With each rise and fall of your breath, you can feel each breath move into your psyche, down through your body, and circulating within. This beautiful purple light is nourishing each of the cells of your entire body, and bringing you focus, direction, empowerment, and healthy transformation.

And as you continue to breathe

I am going to invite you to be creative with your visualization now. There are several animals, mythical and otherwise, associated with Scorpio energy. One of them is a phoenix. A phoenix is a mythological creature of tremendous resilience and fortitude, famously rising from the ashes of the past, stronger than ever. Flying brilliantly in the sky, the phoenix symbolizing our own resilience and resolve. Whatever happens in life, we can use it to be better. We can and we do rise, better than before.

And as you continue to breathe

See yourself as a phoenix now, covered in brilliantly colored feathers and skin, standing on the ground. Around you there might be ashes. There might be memories of the things that didn't always work. There might be disappointments and pain that are a part of any life well lived. And as you look down at these memories, experiences, people, places and things of before, you feel overcome with incredible gratitude. It is all of these memories, experiences, people, places and things of before that are a part of your story, they have made you more wise and loving than you were before. They have brought you to this moment of honesty, perception, and power.

As you continue to breathe this brilliant, vibrant, purple light around and within you

Slowly start to feel your knees bend, as the strength in your legs grow, and you prepare for a lift. See yourself harnessing the power of all you have been, and the power of the vision to carry you forward, prepare your body now.

As you continue to breathe, and with a deep breath in on the exhale, see yourself in your mind's eye, with all your vibrantly colored feathers and skin, feel yourself harness the power of your own muscles and of all the wind, and lift off. Out of the ashes of the past. Out of the memories, experiences, people, places and things of before, who are a part of your story but are no longer weighing you down. See yourself fly up, fly strong, and fly high.

See yourself soar now. High above the past, and moving with love and purpose towards your future.

As you continue to breathe

Affirm to yourself now:

"I know my truth"

"I am resilient, strong, and sure"

"I am better today, for all I learned about myself before"

Gently notice any resistance that might arise, see it for what it is, not arising from love, and let it go. Just put it to the side for now, and gently bring yourself back to your affirmations.

"I have everything that truly matters"

"I know my truth"

"I am resilient, strong, and sure"

Repeat these words to yourself. Feel these words merge with the bright, vibrant purple light, this energy of focus, direction, empowerment, and healthy transformation, flowing within you and flowing through you.

As you continue to breathe

Feel yourself filled with gratitude, for whatever insight has presented itself to you. Whatever vision, whatever feeling. Affirm within you that there is wisdom in this exact moment.

As you continue to breathe

Bring your attention gently to your breath. The feeling of your breath moving through your body, radiating forward from within, through your skin, and throughout your aura.

As you continue to breathe

Bring your attention gently to your breath. The feeling of your breath moving through your nose, your face, and your mouth.

As you continue to breathe

Gently feel yourself being in this present moment more and more. Begin to move your fingers and toes, with an awareness of the parts of your body in contact with a surface.

As you continue to breathe

Come back into this moment, and gently, as you are ready, open your eyes.

As you come back into this moment, and into your conscious awareness...

Jot down any thoughts that you'd like to affirm or remember in a notebook or recording device near you. And before you get up, be sure to thank this space that you were in, knowing that it was exactly as it needed to be.

Sagittarius

Wisdom, Travel, Teaching, Legal Matters, Occasional Awards

Jupiter, Day

Fire Element

Amethyst, Sapphire

Sage, Carnations

Lilac, Mauve, Purple

"The World Is Mine!

The image associated with this archetypal part of the cosmos is the centaur, half beast and half human, who was also an archer. The bow and arrow of this centaur is significant in that it can point and direct its passions outwards towards its aim and is willing to take the chance to see what the arrow will hit. This is the part of us that has not only the confidence of fire, but the ability to change gears and grow as we learn more, and learning in some way is a process this part of us is actively engaged in. Because it is active energy here, there is a restless quality that can be felt right in the soul, a perpetual discontent until this energy is actively engaged in pursuits and goals that are new and encourage enthusiasm. This energy is positive and helpful when it is engaged in exploration, new adventures, philosophical and value considerations, and following up on faith with action.

This is the philosopher vibration. This energy needs to feel like it is always growing, evolving in some way, and learning something new or sharing what it has to give. Fellow fire signs Aries says, "I have this powerful energy." Leo says, "I have this sacred energy that is worthy of being seen." In contrast, the mantra for Sagittarius says, "I am sharing my energy" and does not care what anyone says about it. It is shared for the process of sharing, not so much for the accolades or consequences. It is about finding that thing that resonates within and pursuing it full tilt that makes this part of us most happy.

This is the part of the cosmos that connects with our hips, thighs, liver and sciatic nerve. I think about women, especially myself; what happens to our hips and our thighs? We get cellulite. Why?

Perhaps it has something to do with either caring about what other people think of what we have to share, or perhaps we avoid honoring this energy by not fully sharing our light, our creative selves, in a way that satisfies us. There is a strong need to engage with others, to exchange ideas in an intuitive and in the moment kind of way with this energy. When there is no active engagement with others and enthusiasm around goals and aims, or an active cultivation of new experiences and wisdom, this energy turns in on itself.

The liver helps in the detoxification of our body by releasing what we do not need, but it also produces hormones and helps us digest through the production of bile, which allows us to process a variety of vitamins and fats. The word bile is, interestingly, a synonym for malice, or "bad blood." The liver is also the holder of old wounds, which is why alcohol is so hard on the liver, because it suppresses old wounds. Having a healthy liver is symbolic of maintaining a spirit of optimism, while keeping one's faith that the world is a good and safe place, regardless of life's hardships.

The liver can have an additional association with the sign of Virgo in medical astrology, specifically for its cleansing properties. However, when we explore how Plato understood the liver, we find it fits more precisely with the Sagittarius archetype. Plato spoke of the importance of maintaining a healthy liver due to its value in contributing to prophetic dreams. It is in our dream state that we can allow other aspects of ourselves that provide mental defenses to be brought down enough to let the divinatory value of dreams to come forward. He does warn, however, that it is in consulting another person that an accurate judgment can be made as to their meaning and accuracy. Thus, the liver provides inspiration, but requires sharing to call a verdict on that inspiration. Divination and prophecy are gifts to humanity and represent a personal communication that takes place between the divine and us. Sagittarius is also the sign of the faithful and prophecy, and so the liver, according to Plato, is the seat from which that prophecy may arise.

The sciatic nerve is the largest nerve in our body, and as part of our nervous system (Gemini), is responsible for carrying messages from our lower body to our brain. This nerve most directly symbolizes that the world is a safe place to interact and communicate with. It represents our ability to process and make sense of any new or foreign concept, culture, or experience.

Sagittarius rules the hips and thighs, and there are two major muscle groups in this region of our body. The muscle groups that Sagittarius rules are the quadriceps and hamstrings. The hip flexors are also in this area of the body, and are a part of the skeletal structure (Capricorn). The hamstrings allows us to bend our knees, and are connected to our willingness to engage the world in the pursuit of our ambitions.

The quadriceps, also called quads, is the large muscle that lies in the front and side of the thigh. It contains four heads made up of five distinct muscles that extend from your hip flexors, cascading down to the knees. These muscles allow us to walk, run, or otherwise use our legs. One of the muscles is the *sartorius*, which as the longest muscle in the human body, is consistent with the long journey that is associated with Sagittarius. It begins at the top front of the pelvis and, like a rope, goes down and across, running along the top front and inner part of the lower part of the thigh, assisting us in flexing our knee, as well as flexing, rotating, and abducting our thigh. The second muscle is the *vastus intermedius*, and this muscle runs underneath the *rectus femoris*. The *vastus medialis* and *vastus lateralis* are on the inner and outer thigh respectively.

The *vastus intermedius* and *rectus femoris* symbolizes the enthusiasm with which we engage the world, and how we feel about going out into the larger world to interact and share who we are. The *vastus medialis*, the inner muscle of the thigh, symbolizes the excitement and enthusiasm we actually feel about our lives. The *vastus lateralis*, our outer thigh, symbolizes the polarity and optimism with which we approach other people, and dialogue with them in a spirit of mutual learning and how willing we are to show others that we do not know everything, so that we may learn from them.

The hamstrings consist of three major muscles. The *biceps femoris* is the one that pushes against the skin and is most evident when we build the back of the thighs. Its function is to extend the hip as part of walking. The *semitendinosus* lies next to it in the middle of the leg and helps us straighten our leg. The *semimembranosus* is found in the inner thigh and allows us to straighten and bend the knee.

The *biceps femoris* symbolizes the authenticity of our goals and pursuits, so that they truly are things that ignite our passions and give us "juice." The *semitendinosus* represents "going for it," moving toward our genuine desires, and feeling like we are actively doing our part to have experiences that hold the potential to excite us. The *semimembranosus* represents our most personal feelings of confidence to truly have a life that is fun.

What happens for many people in this part of the body is cellulite. This is energy that pertains to allowing ourselves to have new experiences and exposing ourselves to those things considered foreign. This part of the body speaks to adventure. Cellulite can happen when we are not feeling enthusiastic or stimulated by our experiences in life, when we feel like we are "stuck in a rut," or life becomes otherwise too predictable, and also when we are not actively taking risks, even calculated ones, towards a more fun direction.

It is interesting, but the theory to building the thigh muscles is that they will push against the skin in order to make the cellulite appear less obvious. I find that to be an interesting symbol. As the muscles, the place of inner strength, grow, so too do we find a balance between our enthusiasm and optimism for our goals and our life. Becoming stronger internally, in the very area that allows us to move forward in the world, is symbolic of a healthier relationship with the wider world and with all its experiences contained within an adventure.

Exercises that work the quads are the leg extension. The hamstring extension and reaching dead lift works the hamstring muscles of the body. Yoga poses include the Chair Pose and Warrior Pose.

Meditation for Sagittarius

Lie down or sit in a comfortable position. Close your eyes, or if you prefer, you can choose to start by softly gazing towards an image that feels calming to you. Start to pay attention to your breathing. Don't control it in any way yet, just pay attention to how you are breathing. Feel the breath move through your face,

your nose, your mouth, fill your brain and move deeper into your body.

As you continue to breathe, begin to take your breath deeper. Take a few big breaths in. Feel the strength and power of your breath, filling you with energy and life. Feel your body rise and fall with each breath in. As your body relaxes more, you also can feel yourself more alert, as your mind fills with oxygen.

And as you continue to breathe, bring your attention to the exhale as well. Feel yourself releasing any thoughts of the past or the future. With each exhale, you release any feeling that is not part of this moment, right now. Observe the in and out of your breath. With each exhale you release, with each breath in, you feel more and more aware of this present moment. The present moment is truly all there is. The present moment is where the power is.

As you continue to breathe…

Imagine the air around you as a pure, vibrant, lilac colored light. Notice the shading and beauty of this light. It feels optimistic and expansive. It feels like an energy of adventure. This is the love of learning and the love of wisdom. It is the light of this love that reminds you that life is meant to be a daring adventure, and in believing that great things are possible, they often are. Each moment where you are willing to believe in yourself, in your life, and in your future, you tap into this sacred energy.

On each inhale, you are breathing in this pure, vibrant, lilac colored light.

Imagine this light flooding through your breath, down right into your liver, and then down into your thighs, and through your entire body. Radiating health and nourishing your body. Filling you with this vibrant pure lilac-colored energy.

Become aware of the flow of this breath circulating through your body. See yourself now, glowing from this optimistic, expansive, hopeful, vibrant lilac light, from the inside out. With each rise and fall of your breath, you can feel each breath move into your liver, down through your thighs, and circulating within your entire body. This beautiful lilac light is nourishing each of the cells of your entire body, and bringing your most buoyant, bright, confident, and wise self forward.

And as you continue to breathe

Gently bring your attention to your liver, located on the right side of your body, just below your rib cage. If you are so inspired, you can put one or both of your hands on it now. It was this organ that was believed to hold prophecy to the ancients. The liver is a powerful symbol of cleansing and renewal, putting the hurts of the past behind us so that we can listen to the prophecy of love and wisdom in our own lives.

And as you continue to breathe

Imagine the lilac light, flowing through your body now, as a spinning wheel within your liver, cleansing and releasing any debris you no longer need. Whatever hurts of the past have served their purpose. Bless your experiences of the past and allow yourself to be filled with happiness and love. Starting in your liver, emanating from this spinning wheel of lilac light, and filling your entire body.

As you continue to breathe this brilliant, vibrant, lilac light around and within you

Slowly imagine your liver itself as open to divine wisdom, to divine prophecy. Simply be willing to allow the insights to find you. What is it that will help you on your unique journey towards greater love and greater wisdom? Where is it that you are ready to align with a future of greater love and greater wisdom? What does this future look like? Allow your answers to find you.

As you continue to breathe, and with a deep breath in and then out, see yourself in your mind's eye as a future version of you. Perhaps it is immediately following this meditation, or perhaps another time. You can see yourself radiating love and wisdom. Radiating happiness and enthusiasm for your life and for what's ahead. See your face now, lit up from within, with this very joy.

See yourself, as the answer to what it is that has brought such joy and enthusiasm in your life reveals itself to you now.

As you continue to breathe

Affirm to yourself now:

"My life is constantly leading me towards greater love and greater wisdom"

"I am enthusiastic and excited about what's ahead."

"The world is mine! The world is ours!"

Gently notice any resistance that might arise, see it for what it is, not arising from love, and let it go. Just put it to the side for now, and gently bring yourself back to your affirmations.

"My life is constantly leading me towards greater love and greater wisdom"

"I am enthusiastic and excited about what's ahead."

"The world is mine! The world is ours!"

Repeat these words to yourself. Feel these words merge with the bright, vibrant lilac light. This energy of optimistic, expansive hope is flowing within you and flowing through you.

As you continue to breathe

Feel yourself filled with gratitude, for whatever insight has presented itself to you. Whatever vision, whatever feeling. Affirm within you that there is wisdom in this exact moment.

As you continue to breathe

Bring your attention gently to your breath. The feeling of your breath moving through your body, radiating forward from within, through your liver and thighs, and throughout your aura.

As you continue to breathe

Bring your attention gently to your breath. The feeling of your breath moving through your nose, your face, and your mouth.

As you continue to breathe…

Gently feel yourself being in this present moment more and more. Begin to move your fingers and toes, with an awareness of the parts of your body in contact with a surface.

As you continue to breathe

Come back into this moment, and gently, as you are ready, open your eyes.

As you come back into this moment, and into your conscious awareness…

Jot down any thoughts that you'd like to affirm or remember in a notebook or recording device near you. And before you get up, be sure to thank this space that you were in, knowing that it was exactly as it needed to be.

Capricorn

Success, Achievement, Recognition for Contribution

Saturn, Day

Earth Element

Onyx, Obsidian

Nightshade, Hemlock

Brown, Grey, Violet

"I Am A Success!"

This is the part of the cosmos that has to do with achievement in society, respect, and the father or fatherhood. Capricorn energy is about honoring the established structures that are already in place, and also about establishing wealth. It is strong, stable and willing to do the work that is required and take the steps that are needed to make that dream happen, trusting that when it follows through with the process, a place of respectability will be assured, no matter how long it takes, or how arduous the work may be. There is an understanding that time is something that we all have, but it does go by, so use it well and leave a mark.

The Capricorn part of us shows an area of life where we are likely to make a choice that is based on established mores, and it will control our energy so that it sustains over a period of time. This is the part of us that comes from a realistic place and with an understanding that the end matters just as much as the start. Desires are backed up with action, and that is how self-respect is earned. This is the part of us that needs respect and to feel like we are building authority. The spiritual attributes correlate to the joints, particularly the knees, and also the skeletal system.

We have several joints in our body, including at the shoulder, elbow, hands, wrists (Gemini), hips, pelvis (Sagittarius), knees (Capricorn), ankles (Aquarius), feet (Pisces), as well as the jaw (Taurus) and spine (Leo). Connective tissues, ligaments, and cartilage surround them. Joints essentially connect our bones at places of movement. The knees themselves correlate to the Capricorn part of the cosmos and us, while the other joints take other parts of us into account, for the spiritual qualities they represent, and how they contribute to, or meet, our ambition and the attainment of our career aims.

Our skeletal system comprises of a frame of bones, within which is the marrow, around which the entirety of our physical bodies, including all tissue, is built. It provides protection for some of our organs. In all, we are comprised of 206 bones.

Joints are symbolic of our willingness to engage different parts of various skills and ourselves in the achievement of our ambitions. They also symbolize our perceived ability to accomplish our goals, and how we employ the various skills and archetypes we believe we have access to when trying to achieve our career aims. When problems arise in our joints and bones, it can indicate a feeling that some authority that you hold is not being acknowledged or respected. Sometimes, forgiveness of the father is required. In addition, this has to do with being respected, and the joint signaled would speak to what skills need to come forth to address our forgiveness or need for respect.

For example, the joints in the shoulder, elbow, wrists, and hands correlate to how we use our perceptions and communication (Gemini) to address our higher aims. The joints in our jaw and neck connect to manifesting and creating monetary gain for ourselves (Taurus) in line with the contribution or legacy desires we have. The joints in the spine are connected to our feelings of worthiness (Leo) to achieve our goals. The joints in our hips and pelvis relate to exposing ourselves to new ideas, cultures, or experiences (Sagittarius) that could allow us to fulfill our goals.

The feet correlate with how our ambitions effectively integrate our inspiration (Pisces), and the ankles align our career goals with a desire to contribute to the collective, while maintaining an individual identity (Aquarius).

While we cannot control outer circumstances, we need to feel that the actions we are taking can be considered respectable, because ensuring our respectability can ease any discomfort. In addition, Capricorn rules societal structures, and where we feel like we are not contributing or interacting with the structure, or where we feel like we are not with rising through the ranks quickly enough, problems can show up. Capricorn also rules the father or our main paternal figure. Issues of forgiveness surrounding your dad can manifest in the knees and bones.

Knees are also symbolic of the balance between doing all we can to manifest our destiny, and staying open in trust that things are unfolding as they should. I remember a time when I was driving myself crazy trying to make something happen in my career. I could not hold on to that emotion for too long before my knees started to bother me. I came to realize that I was not expressing my trust in a higher plan for my life and was carrying the burden all on my own. I got into my career because it was fun and a privilege to share my spirituality, but I had lost touch with that motivation and made it about success. My focus had to change. I had to reel myself back to the moment and away from simply achieving a goal. There is nothing wrong with ambition, I thoroughly believe that, but it must not exist at the expense of the process. The process is where the magic, joy, and power are.

Having faith that everything is unfolding as it should, taking responsibility, and trusting the process returned my knees to their rightful strength.

There are places in our life where we settle for mediocrity. Whether it is in our relationships, finances, work situations, and especially where it comes to the standing we occupy in society, sometimes it seems hard just to say and claim what it is that you believe you deserve and then go for it with everything in you. Here's the trick, find the joy in the process so that you are not attached to the outcome. Sure, you want your efforts to be meaningful and count for something, but the sheer joy of going for gold in the faith that you will achieve it is what moves us away from mediocrity. Being willing to dream and think big of our lives, being willing to make it big no matter what our specialty may be, to demand and command respect from ourselves, from the people around us, and from the world at large; this is what it is to reject mediocrity.

However, there is a fine balance. Ultimately, it is about what is happening in the internal place that matters most. It is about the inner state of respect that can be reflected in our circumstances. When we demand that we treat ourselves with the utmost respect and ask for that from those that surround us, then the world often responds in kind with respectful interactions. When we respect ourselves, we also do not keep people who are not respectful in our life and we in turn show respect to others.

Attaining the balance involves being flexible. The knee is one of the most sensitive spots on the body, and a place where athletes who push the growing strength and speed of their body on a path that will culminate with the infusion of spirit and matter that is needed to lead them to triumph, experience the most issues. They strive for excellence each time they participate in their sport, but excellence is not only a matter of success on a playing field. There is the internal feeling of success that is also important, and an appreciation of the fact that what may not appear to be success on the surface actually is, or will be, once seen in the fullness of time and hindsight.

An athlete can give it their all on the field and still not win the game, but they may also never know how or why a victory for the other team was so crucial or important, and why it had to be so. Demanding a win, demanding their personal best, without faith and release of the final outcome, leads to inflexibility. Success will need to be defined in much more personal terms, in terms that match effort and spirit, while remaining flexible on the outcome. One loss does not mean that the season is lost forever, and God's delays are not denials. But there is something to be said for being a vessel and letting your Higher Power work through you, while doing your best and changing course as new information reveals itself.

One of the major ways to release expectations is to have fun! When the end goal of success becomes more important than the joy of the experience, then we lose our sense of fun. If you experience problems in the knees, consider making fun a higher priority in your life. If it is another joint that is causing you problems, consider what skills your spiritual attributes can utilize, as indicated by the part of the cosmos that part of your body is leading you to, so that you can achieve your aims and yet, make it a fun process, grounded in the knowledge that every effort made is meaningful and is a part of achieving and living your destiny.

The bones are the basic structure that everything else is built around in our physical body. Plato felt that our bones held our reason; our marrow allows mind and body to unite. In fact, the marrow is what is created first in a human being, and contains within it the seed of the soul of all humanity, which is common to all of us. The bonier an area of the body is, the more energy of reason it contains. Experiment with this. Consider your body, and regardless of your size, observe your most bony parts. What archetype do they correspond to? Is this an area of life that you consider yourself as most rational?

It is also said of the bones that they are the only things about our physical selves that lasts forever; it can remain for millions of years after we die. There is something immortal about our skeletal structure. Capricorn, as a sign, rules the legacy we leave. The question to ask here is "what is my legacy?" Go on to build on that. Where we feel that we are creating a legacy that we do not desire to live, or leave behind, we will have to address that within ourselves.

Sometimes we think that we have to do something big to create a lasting legacy. We think we have to be very rich, very famous, or very influential. Those things are all wonderful, but ultimately, each one of us leaves a legacy of some kind anytime we give and show love to one another. That is really all it takes. We just cannot know how one small moment of kindness can change the trajectory of someone's life forever, when a small, seemingly inconsequential moment may come up in someone's mind and be just the meaningful experience from their past they needed to begin to move into a more loving or empowered future. We cannot know, with our limited vision, how grand and mysterious the Universe is, and how a higher power uses us in the smallest of ways, ways that make the biggest difference to one or many more people. In some way, every day, no matter what we are doing or how we live, we are shaping and affecting our legacy and leaving the world changed as a result of our existence.

This energy has a strong, practical, initiative quality to it. It is about the enterprising nature needed to achieve one's legacy, even within an organization or established structure. If the effort never begins, the journey never starts, and nothing gets done. Capricorn energy is one of focus on achievement. The trick is the focus has to come from a place of focus on living in alignment with a higher will, as opposed to focus on the desires of the emotions or fears. Emotional intensity and desire are wonderful, but not if you miss out on life in the process. Engage with life, engage with all facets of it and incorporate new experiences, even if they seem to have nothing to do with your goals. In addition, focusing on knowledge of doing your part in a greater will, and trusting your destiny, is what helps us learn and ease any discomfort.

Yoga poses include the Extended Triangle Pose and the Half Moon Pose. The Mountain Pose is also powerfully symbolic for the mountain goat, one of the animals emblematic of Capricorn.

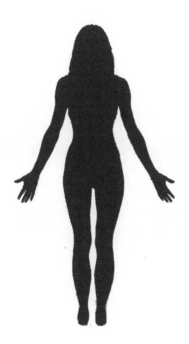

Meditation for Capricorn

Lie down or sit in a comfortable position. Close your eyes, or if you prefer, you can choose to start by softly gazing towards an image that feels calming to you. Start to pay attention to your breathing. Don't control it in any way yet, just pay attention to how you are breathing. Feel the breath move through your face,

your nose, your mouth, fill your brain and move deeper into your body.

As you continue to breathe, begin to take your breath deeper. Take a few big breaths in. Feel the strength and power of your breath, filling you with energy and life. Feel your body rise and fall with each breath in. As your body relaxes more, you also can feel yourself more alert, as your mind fills with oxygen.

And as you continue to breathe, bring your attention to the exhale as well. Feel yourself releasing any thoughts of the past or the future. With each exhale, you release any feeling that is not part of this moment, right now. Observe the in and out of your breath. With each exhale you release, with each breath in, you feel more and more aware of this present moment. The present moment is truly all there is. The present moment is where the power is.

As you continue to breathe…

Imagine the air around you as a pure, vibrant, earthy light. Notice the shading and beauty of this light. It feels grounding and practical. It feels like an energy of ambition and success. This is the love of free-will, used with wisdom and purpose. It is the light of this love that reminds you that life is meant to be lived integrated with our practical surroundings, and in believing in our own abilities, we can transform our lived circumstances for the better. Each moment where you are willing to believe in a vision you have for you life, and take action in support of that outcome, you tap into this sacred energy.

On each inhale, you are breathing in this pure, vibrant, earthy light.

Imagine this light flooding through your breath, into your body, and right into your bones. See your joints and your skeleton radiating with health, as this light nourishes your body, from the deepest core, out.

And as you continue to breathe

I will invite you to imagine yourself, as you are sitting or lying down right now, next to a tree. Take note of the strength, age, beauty, and majesty of this tree. Take a moment now to consider how this tree, now providing you with shade, comfort, and connection, became so majestic. There might have been times of stress and reach, but more often than not, this tree allowed itself to surrender to its natural inclination to grow, continuously to higher and higher heights. Continuously, growing more strong and sturdy in its place.

And as you continue to breathe

Contemplate yourself and how you are like this tree. At times consciously, at times naturally, at times with ebb and at other with flow, but constantly moving forward, upwards, and knowing yourself as more majestic than you have before.

As you continue to breathe this brilliant, vibrant, earthy light around and within you

Think of yourself now as this tree, with your head representing the very top leaves of the beautiful, majestic expression of nature that you are. As you grow to the sky, you are looking up. Imagine yourself looking upwards, and realizing, that you are moving towards something in the distance. It is a vision of yourself, at a place of achievement, as you uniquely define it. As you grow closer towards this vision, you can see yourself having something you wanted, something you have worked towards. It might be a thing, an experience, a credential or a position. Whatever it is that is uniquely for you, you know it is you, enjoying your success. See yourself in a place of acquisition and celebration now, having the thing you told the Universe you wanted, with your work, your vision, and your effort.

As you continue to breathe, and with a deep breath in and then out, see yourself in your mind's eye as this future version of you, but it is here now. You are living it. You have earned it.

And as you continue to breathe

Affirm to yourself now:

"My life is constantly leading me to align with a higher, more loving vision for my life"

"My unique definition of success is the only one that matters"

"The Universe has a divine destiny for me, greater than anything I could plan for myself."

Gently notice any resistance that might arise, see it for what it is, not arising from love, and let it go. Just put it to the side for now, and gently bring yourself back to your affirmations.

"My life is constantly leading me to align with a higher, more loving vision for my life"

"My unique definition of success is the only one that matters"

"The Universe has a divine destiny for me, greater than anything I could plan for myself."

Repeat these words to yourself. Feel these words merge with the bright, vibrant earthy light, this energy of ambition, success, alignment with your life purpose, flowing within you and flowing through you.

As you continue to breathe

Feel yourself filled with gratitude, for whatever insight has presented itself to you. Whatever vision, whatever feeling. Affirm within you that there is success in this exact moment.

As you continue to breathe

Bring your attention gently to your breath. The feeling of your breath moving through your body, radiating forward from within, from your bones, though your body, and throughout your aura.

As you continue to breathe

Bring your attention gently to your breath. The feeling of your breath moving through your nose, your face, and your mouth.

As you continue to breathe

Gently feel yourself being in this present moment more and more. Begin to move your fingers and toes, with an awareness of the parts of your body in contact with a surface.

As you continue to breathe

Come back into this moment, and gently, as you are ready, open your eyes.

As you come back into this moment, and into your conscious awareness...

Jot down any thoughts that you'd like to affirm or remember in a notebook or recording device near you. And before you get up, be sure to thank this space that you were in, knowing that it was exactly as it needed to be.

Aquarius

Authentic Expression, Individuality, Rebellion, Freedom

Saturn Night, Uranus

Air Element

Zircon, Amethyst

Valerian, Clove

Bright Electric Blues, Greens, Purples, Iridescent Colors

"I Am Free to Be Me"

This is the part of the sky that is connected to the archetype of invention, independence, and idiosyncrasy. This sign can be very analytical and get high on the mental plane, preoccupied with thought and new, novel, inspired ideas. It is also inspiration and inner authority. The inventiveness and brilliance can be amplified, as is the unpredictability. There is a strong dichotomy here, as represented in its glyphs of two waves. On the one hand, it is a sign that cares about humanitarianism and friendship, but it is also a very individualistic sign and highly values their own space.

This is a sign with a strong duality, and while it's connected with the collective at its core, once establishing itself it becomes highly individualistic with a very strong voice of inner authority. There is a strong emphasis placed on mind, thoughts, a strong sense of self, and a deep commitment to the inner voice. There is a tendency to go against the grain simply for the sake of it, or to display rebellion before the lesson that the revolution has to happen from within is mastered, and living life in accordance to your own wisdom is an act of revolution. This is the archetype that rules astrology, because it brings intuition and sciences together. The mantra is "We all have our own truth, and I know my truth."

The Aquarian energy corresponds to our calves, shins, ankles, and circulatory health. One of calf muscles is called the *gastrocnemius*. It is comprised of two parts, an inner and outer, and connects to the Achilles tendon. The other calf muscle is the *soleus*, which lies behind the *gastrocnemius*. The calf connects the knees to our heels, and allows us to stand, walk, and jump. In fact, we can see it working when involved in these activities. The *soleus* helps the calf do its function, but most importantly, it allows us to stand with our legs straight. It lies just behind, in support of the calf.

The Achilles heel, also called Achilles tendon, acts as an intermediary between the calf muscle and the plantar muscles, which are a group of muscles in the foot. It is found in the back of the ankle. The ankle itself is a joint, which connects our entire leg with our foot.

The idiosyncratic and random nature of this energy is reflected in the unpredictable way that cramps can arise in this part of the body. The calves symbolize our connection to our own unique inner voice, the inner authority that is at the foundation of new age spirituality, and our willingness to honor that voice. How much we consult it, defer to it, honor it, and ultimately trust it, will show up in these muscles. The *soleus* is much more connected to that deep inner knowledge that is felt in the gut as energy. The *gastrocnemius* muscles are representative of our ability to belong and get along within groups, alliances, and friendships. The inner calf speaks to maintaining a sense of self-identity within a group, while the outer head speaks to our ability to be part of the collective in a humanitarian manner, seeing ourselves as part of a group identity, as one of them, in empathy.

The Achilles heel has a famous Greek myth associated with it. Achilles was a powerful warrior who could win any battle, but had one very vulnerable spot. Aquarius as an archetype oversees this part of the body. The archetypal energy is very detached on the surface with its strong focus on rationality and the mind. However, this is a type of control. Once that detachment has been transcended and things felt deeply, surrender is required, and the loss of control required in surrender leads to vulnerability. The Achilles heel is a symbol of caring to the point of vulnerability, especially when we would rather be more detached and rational. This is when problems can creep in. The key is to allow ourselves to care deeply while maintaining a connection to the rational part of us so that we can see things from a more detached place. Feelings and emotions are very good. So is vulnerability when it is properly placed. It is most properly placed with people who we can trust, through the past actions they have shown us. Also being vulnerable with ourselves is safe, especially when we know we can trust ourselves.

The ankles are a joint connection, our collective identity with our understanding of ourselves within the collective unconscious (Pisces). They are the bridge between our compassion (Pisces) and humanitarian efforts. They are symbolic of turning feelings of connection (Pisces) with rational thought that can allow us to make notable contributions to the world that can actually create positive change in the lives of large groups of people. Added to this is the fact that the ankles are a joint and symbolize turning these connections into achievement in the world, especially in our career endeavors (Capricorn). The ankles are symbolic of turning deep understandings to abstract concepts, ideas, and efforts that can change the world and allow us to create a legacy in the process.

The *soleus* adds size and bulk to this part of the body when it is developed, while the *gastrocnemius* creates striations and a diamond shape. Exercises to strengthen this area include calf raises, which are done at different angles to build the parts where you feel the need for stimulation. Ankle circles keep the joint flexible, and Achilles stretches work the tendon.

The shin is a bone that extends at the front of the leg from the knee to ankle, also called the tibia. The shins symbolize our willingness and comfort with taking a stand that asserts our independence, especially in the face of opposing group consciousness, and especially when this understanding is perceived to affect or influence our ambitions (Capricorn). It is also related to wanting your independence recognized and respected, even if it means going against the grain of a group, collective, or shared identity you belong to. It is being OK with not being a part of the collective head in thought, and wanting your unique contributions acknowledged.

Our circulatory system helps keep our body moving and flowing by carrying our blood, nutrients, hormones, and waste to their appropriate organs for processing. The circulatory system also stabilizes the temperature of our body and our inner environment. Cold hands and feet indicate poor circulation.

Our circulation speaks to how well we are able to rely on our inner authority and maintain a strong, personal identity while maintaining our alliances to various collectives. Our circulation is responsible for homeostasis- a term that means a stable inner environment. Our circulation is symbolic of feeling an inner stability and spiritual consistency that comes from self-trust, regardless of how chaotic the people around us may be.

The single most important thing that can be done to strengthen the circulatory system is cardio exercise, which encourages movement of fluids in our body, revitalizes our blood with oxygen, and encourages our body to equalize its temperature as our internal heat rises.

Yoga poses include the Half Frog Pose and the High Lunge, Crescent Variation.

Meditation for Aquarius

Lie down or sit in a comfortable position. Close your eyes, or if you prefer, you can choose to start by softly gazing towards an image that feels calming to you. Start to pay attention to your breathing. Don't control it in any way yet, just pay attention to how you are breathing. Feel the breath move through your face,

your nose, your mouth, fill your brain and move deeper into your body.

As you continue to breathe, begin to take your breath deeper. Take a few big breaths in. Feel the strength and power of your breath, filling you with energy and life. Feel your body rise and fall with each breath in. As your body relaxes more, you also can feel yourself more alert, as your mind fills with oxygen.

And as you continue to breathe, bring your attention to the exhale as well. Feel yourself releasing any thoughts of the past or the future. With each exhale, you release any feeling that is not part of this moment, right now. Observe the in and out of your breath. With each exhale you release, with each breath in, you feel more and more aware of this present moment. The present moment is truly all there is. The present moment is where the power is.

As you continue to breathe

Imagine the air around you as a pure, vibrant, electric-blue light. Notice the shading and beauty of this light. It feels authentic and original. It feels like an energy of individuality and rebellion. This is the love of all things new; new ideas, new experiences, new intuitions, and new ways of expressing yourself. It is the light of this love that reminds you that life is meant to be filled with growth and change, and the most rewarding lives are those that are well lived, true to your heart and true to yourself. Each moment where you are willing to trust yourself and be spontaneous in support of your most authentic self, you tap into this sacred energy.

On each inhale, you are breathing in this pure, vibrant, electric-blue light. On the exhale, this light fills your aura with an energy of intelligence, awakening, and excitement. Sit with this flow of breath now. Imagine this light flooding through your breath, into your body, right down into your calves and your ankles. See your calves and ankles radiating with health, as this light nourishes your entire body, from the deepest core, out.

And as you continue to breathe

Gently bring your attention to your lower legs, your calves and ankles in particular. It is the ankles that hold the symbol of the Achilles heel. This is the part of you that feels especially open to vulnerabilities. Whatever your unique Achilles heel may be, imagine yourself now, symbolically, holding it in your hands. And as you gaze upon the thing within you that has felt especially vulnerable, whether it is an experience in your past or a part of your present, or perhaps what you fear in your future, as you gaze upon it now, see it glowing with the pure, vibrant, electric-blue light you are breathing now.

And as you continue to breathe

Consider how it is this very thing, your Achilles heel, that has come into your life with great wisdom and purpose. There have been good things to come from this vulnerability. Perhaps it has helped you feel safe. Perhaps it has led to you becoming a more compassionate person. As you sit with your Achilles heel in front of you now, ask it what are some of the higher outcomes of its presence in your life now.

As you continue to breathe this pure, vibrant, electric-blue light around and within you

Give this very part of you, this beautiful Achilles heel in your hands now, a big burst of love and gratitude. Now that you see the wisdom and beauty of this part of your story, feel overcome with the love of this perspective, the love of this part of you. Give this most vulnerable part of you a big hug in your mind's eye now.

And as you continue to breathe

Affirm to yourself now:

"I am free to be my most authentic self"

"My vulnerability is my super power"

"All parts of me and of my story make me the unique expression of divine light that I am"

Gently notice any resistance that might arise, see it for what it is, not arising from love, and let it go. Just put it to the side for now, and gently bring yourself back to your affirmations.

"I am free to be my most authentic self"

"My vulnerability is my super power"

"All parts of me and of my story make me the unique expression of divine light that I am"

Repeat these words to yourself. Feel these words merge with the pure, vibrant, electric-blue light around and within you. Feel the energy of authenticity, individuality, and the full embrace and acceptance of all parts of you, flowing within you and flowing through you.

As you continue to breathe

Feel yourself filled with gratitude, for whatever insight has presented itself to you. Whatever vision, whatever feeling. Affirm within you that there is honesty in this exact moment.

As you continue to breathe

Bring your attention gently to your breath. The feeling of your breath moving through your body, radiating forward from within, from your bones, though your body, and throughout your aura.

As you continue to breathe

Bring your attention gently to your breath. The feeling of your breath moving through your nose, your face, and your mouth.

As you continue to breathe

Gently feel yourself being in this present moment more and more. Begin to move your fingers and toes, with an awareness of the parts of your body in contact with a surface.

As you continue to breathe

Come back into this moment, and gently, as you are ready, open your eyes.

As you come back into this moment, and into your conscious awareness…

Jot down any thoughts that you'd like to affirm or remember in a notebook or recording device near you. And before you get up, be sure to thank this space that you were in, knowing that it was exactly as it needed to be.

Pisces

Communion, Visions, Arts, Poetry, Music, Healing

Jupiter Night, Neptune

Water Element

Aquamarine, Amethyst

Lotus, Water Lily

Violet, Sea Green, Clear Blue

"I Am One with All"

Considered by some as the most spiritual part of the cosmos (though, as a side note, I think all of the cosmos, and therefore our body, is spiritual), probably because of the very compassionate and ethereal nature of this archetype, this is the subconscious and the dream state, and people who are very strongly allied to this energy may look as though they are connected to some other realm by the dreaminess in their eyes. This is the part of us that can be very idealistic and spiritual, having a wondrous belief of the world and in possibilities, and even feels aligned with psychic understandings and mystical expressions, especially in art as an expression of the divine. There is communion on some level desired with a mystical source. The mantra is "aligned with a higher purpose."

The parts of the body this archetype corresponds to are the feet, toes, lymphatic system, and adipose tissue. Our feet are very complex, with a variety of bones, muscles, tissues, and very strong skin at their sole. The feet are literally symbolic of the place in which we stand. Our feet carry us, root us, and give us a sense of place. Their connection to this most mystical archetype suggests that we know where we stand once we are connected to the spiritual energy that permeates us all.

Pisces rules escapism, and where this energy is in excess, it can find us escaping from reality. This is also the area of the sky ruling addictive behavior, compulsion, and intoxication. Again, excess can lead to problems in this area. This is when we are not dealing with reality, not grounded or rooted in the earth and dealing with things in a practical way. Feet provide support and allow us to walk through our lives with presence, and when we lack presence, or feel like we are not standing in ourselves, it is indicative of problems in this area. There is a disconnect from the physical that happens in this place, so this part of the body can ask for our attention when we are not living in an integrated, holistic way, and instead living in esoteric realms. The spiritual pervades the physical, but it is not the only thing there is.

It is interesting that this part of the sky rules adipose tissue, also known as the fat tissue, a part of every healthy body. Fat has a purpose in our body. It provides a store of energy so that we can survive in extreme circumstances. Fat also provides insulation that protects our organs and bones. These are the benefits of fatty tissue. It is a part of us. It is deserving of being owned and blessed. If you feel you have too much of it, then consider how much protection you actually need, and what you may be protecting yourself from.

The lymph nodes filter lymphatic fluid in our body, fluid being symbolic of emotion. A problem with the lymph nodes indicates an imbalance of emotion and also a desire to insulate oneself from reality. The lymphatic system allows our immune system to kick in and works with it. It is the fluid we need so that we can be protected from outside influences that could harm us. Too much of it can indicate a feeling or over-concern that outside influences are too close. An overwhelming need to keep outside influences at bay could be indicated because we feel that external forces may harm us. The lymphatic fluid also allows us to digest fats and fatty acids, making insulation a process that need not create isolation, but rather, those things that come up in our lives that lead us to feel we would like to be insulated are processed and integrated.

The time of day that this archetype speaks to is the moment before sunrise. We are either deep in sleep or deep in our dream. All is still and no one has awakened. This energy is about that place before we are awake; that dream state that can feel as if we traveled to another place. It is the moment before life stirs, the womb and the gestation period, before the birth. It is the unconscious, the place of suppressed experiences and the source of fears. It is also the shadow and all the things we deny as a part of us. However, the thing is, it is all in an emotional realm and represented in a part of our body that we do not even see. It is the part of us that comes up in dreams, when our defenses are down.

The idea that Pisces rules altered states of conscious and other realms of understanding is a part of what makes life a magical place to be. When this energy is healthy, it is a life that feels inspired, mystical, and a personal connection with a Higher Power, felt in every aspect of life and in the emotions. Too much of this energy makes us ignore the very tangible, real, physical realm. Balancing this energy requires meditation in regular doses, but not living in a meditative state. When it's too much Piscean energy, which shows up as too much fat and water in our bodies, or inadequate amounts (which can lead to a hyper emphasis only on the tangible), it can lead to an absence or painful problems in these fluids and cells. A healthy Pisces energy means that we keep our feet on the ground but our head in the sky.

Yoga poses to engage Piscean energy include The Warrior Pose and The Reclining Hand To Big Toe Pose.

Meditation for Pisces

Lie down or sit in a comfortable position. Close your eyes, or if you prefer, you can choose to start by softly gazing towards an image that feels calming to you. Start to pay attention to your breathing. Don't control it in any way yet, just pay attention to how you are breathing. Feel the breath move through your face, your nose, your mouth, fill your brain and move deeper into your body.

As you continue to breathe, begin to take your breath deeper. Take a few big breaths in. Feel the strength and power of your breath, filling you with energy and life. Feel your body rise and fall with each breath in. As your body relaxes more, you also can feel yourself more alert, as your mind fills with oxygen.

And as you continue to breathe, bring your attention to the exhale as well. Feel yourself releasing any thoughts of the past or the future. With each exhale, you release any feeling that is not part of this moment, right now. Observe the in and out of your breath. With each exhale you release, with each breath in, you feel more and more aware of this present moment. The present moment is truly all there is. The present moment is where the power is.

As you continue to breathe

Imagine the air around you as a pure, vibrant, healing iridescent sea-green light. Notice the shading and beauty of this light. It feels inviting, compassionate and comforting. It feels like an energy of healing and connection. This is the love of communion, and recognizing our inherent connection to everyone and everything. It is the light of this love that reminds you that life is meant to be lived interconnected, and not only for ourselves. It is in the giving of ourselves that we find whom it is we really are. It is in sacrifice that we can gain the things we are most proud of. It is in kindness that we ourselves are most eased.

On each inhale, you are breathing in this pure, vibrant, healing iridescent sea-green light. On the exhale, feel your entire body relax more and more.

And as you continue to breathe

Gently bring your attention to your lower legs, your feet in particular. Consider the feet as a metaphor now, in your life, and all they represent. It is your feet that have supported you on your journey through life. All the pathways you have walked and the experiences you've had. The places you've been and all the times when, because of where your feet took you, you found yourself in other people. Because of the places your feet took you, you found genuine empathy and the renewal of compassion.

And as you continue to breathe

Send your feet a burst of gratitude. Send them love for where they have taken you. Feel excitement and love for where they have yet to take you still.

As you continue to breathe this pure, vibrant, healing iridescent sea-green light around and within you, gently turn your mind's eye to the feeling of this very light all around you. Feel the easy way it moves through you and around you.

Slowly, as you continue to bask in this pure, vibrant, healing iridescent sea-green light, you realize that it is actually water. You are now being carried by a beautiful body of water, holding your body with its strength, moving freely around and through you, with ease and calm

And as you continue to breath, enjoying the feeling of being immersed in water, gently lean your head back slightly, so that the water is now covering your ears. This grand body of water has something to tell you, some wisdom to share. And as you allow this immense and healing body of water to hold you with its strength, listening to these calm and healing waters, listen to its' wisdom it desires to share now.

And as you continue to breathe, affirm to yourself now:

"I am one with all."

"I am compassionate and kind to all I have ever been, all I am, and all I ever will be."

"I move with the ebb and flow of my life."

Gently notice any resistance that might arise, see it for what it is, not arising from love, and let it go. Just put it to the side for now, and gently bring yourself back to your affirmations.

"I am one with all."

"I am compassionate and kind to all I have ever been, all I am, and all I ever will be."

"I move with the ebb and flow of my life."

Repeat these words to yourself. Feel these words merge with the pure, vibrant, healing iridescent sea green light, this energy of compassion, healing, and acceptance, flowing within you and flowing through you.

As you continue to breathe

Feel yourself filled with gratitude, for whatever insight has presented itself to you. Whatever vision, whatever feeling. As you gently begin to prepare to leave, give thanks to the water around you and within, for carrying you with its strength and granting you its wisdom, knowing that this wisdom is always there.

As you continue to breathe

Bring your attention gently to your breath. The feeling of your breath moving through your body, radiating forward from within, from your feet, though your body, and throughout your aura.

As you continue to breathe

Bring your attention gently to your breath. The feeling of your breath moving through your nose, your face, and your mouth.

As you continue to breathe

Gently feel yourself being in this present moment more and more. Begin to move your fingers and toes, with an awareness of the parts of your body in contact with a surface.

As you continue to breathe

Come back into this moment, and gently, as you are ready, open your eyes.

As you come back into this moment, and into your conscious awareness...

Jot down any thoughts that you'd like to affirm or remember in a notebook or recording device near you. And before you get up, be sure to thank this space that you were in, knowing that it was exactly as it needed to be.

Conclusion: Visiting Ares

I stepped into Ancient Agora, the sacred site in Old Athens that was the stomping grounds of Socrates. I walked around and saw the platform where so many of his famous conversations, documented in the writings of Plato, were given. The whole surrounding site was massive, encompassing several temples and functional structures of a time long past. Though all that was left were ruins and rubble, the local tourist board had taken care to properly note what each segment was used for, as well as document pictorial reconstructions of what these buildings must have looked like over 2500 years ago.

I was searching for the temple of Ares. Having done my first ever written work as a graduate student on his symbols and mythology, I felt that it was his energy that was particularly relevant to my spiritual explorations of that time in my life. I was eager to find him and be in the exact space where people many centuries earlier had come to offer thanks, gifts and pleas for assistance. I was so eager that wandering around in hopes of finding his altar proved impossible, and I asked directions whenever I could, all in the hopes of moving a bit closer to Ares.

During my search I was stopped in my tracks by three high columns placed closely together, signifying the entrance to an ancient structure. On top of each were the statues of different figures. They appeared as deities to me. Even after centuries of abandon and inattention, the attention given to detail was still unmistakably revealed in the stone and marble. I was surrounded by beautiful mountainous views in the distance, and temples with representations of their significant Gods and Goddesses, representing the Greek pantheon, all around me.

I stopped to touch some of the rubble in the hopes of gaining a deeper understanding through my fingers, and to deeply engrave the commitment I have made to myself to live this path of astrology and honoring the ancient energies.

As if in a trance, I returned to my senses and remembered that I needed to find Ares. I turned away from the collective of tourists to leave and walked five steps. I had to stop because the late summer sun was searing in this part of the world. I turned my head to find a place to sit, and there was the sign I had yearned for. The single most important thing that had brought me to Greece. A stone carved with words in both English and Greek that said "Temple of Ares." I exhaled and then I smiled. As if this place was waiting for me, I saw a small groove and sat down. I said "thank you" out loud.

Ares is a character who, like all of us, is complex and varied. He has parts of him that are counterintuitive, reckless, and selfish, but also a side that is focused, deeply transformative, and action oriented. This is not transformation that stays on the intellectual or esoteric levels; it is change that is backed up with action.

Ares captures the phrase "I am a spiritual being having an earthly experience." To focus only on one side of Ares, to focus only on the spiritual is to deny that we are embodied being with a body that requires our attention. To place overemphasis on the earthly experience leads to suffering and imbalance. Both need to be acknowledged and integrated if we are to have meaningful, complete lives.

On trips to both Italy and Greece, I was struck by the contrast of these places, considering their shared connection to ancient religions, which are still practiced, albeit on very covert and sometimes unconscious levels. Both places have connections to Gods and Goddesses that are still named when we speak of the planets, deities that are still invoked every time we consider the sacredness of the sky. This is perhaps one of the uneasy places of compromise, a compromise that has allowed these Gods to survive to this day within largely monotheistic cultures. The acceptance of a prime mover, or a singular guiding principal, has allowed the reconciliation to the present day.

Visiting these places was significant in many respects. It allows for a deeper appreciation of what we have experienced as a human community. It allows for an understanding that we are all part of a lineage of our own. We have our physical ancestry that we know through our families. There is our emotional ancestry, as everything that we have ever felt has been felt by other people the world over. We are common in our human emotions, and the ancient Gods and Goddesses indicate this as well. We also have a shared intellectual heritage. The thoughts and intellectual considerations we have hold a history and a line of development that can be traced back. Both these places are special and sacred, and speak to the ancestry that we all have, that shape and guide who we choose to become today.

Though I remain a work in progress, and my life has shown me that, for me, true change involves what appear to be setbacks and plateaus, I know I am better today for having cultivated this relationship with the astrological sky than I was before he came into my active, conscious awareness. I look forward to our continued friendship and how it may change and empower me next.

Acknowledgments and Gratitudes

Thank You to my Fabulous Friends, Fans, Superstars, Clients, and Students. Your trust means so much to me. Sharing this journey with you makes it that much more rewarding.

Thank you to my family, spiritual and physical. My amazing parents Shahnaz and Saif, my brother Fareed and Sister-In-Law Jenn. My many extended family members, especially my aunt Shireen, whose wisdom shows up in my work almost every day. To Manuel and Biggie, my little family that means so much to me. Thank You all for your unconditional love, always.

Yaviz Basalamah is the artist who designed the cover of this book. I love your art Yaviz! I am forever grateful you share your creativity with me and with the world.

Thanks to my astrologer friend Andy for his inspiration, encouragement, support and editorial help, even when he and his Galactic Centerish Sagittarius Mars are ranting that they don't agree with anybody's ideas (including mine!). Andy is one of my very best astrology friends. We are often seen hanging out at astrology conferences together.

To my amazing Patrons, who were a source of love, support, and encouragement, I thank you. Special thanks go to Gloria Novaa, Ruth Ann Santiago, Terra Tecchio, and Susan Farmer. My heartfelt gratitude to you all.

My amazing astrological community! My own personal Jupiter, Michael Barwick. The late, great Donna Van Toen, who I forever credit with my very first big breaks, placing me where I am today through the many blessings she granted me. There are many others in the astrology community who have my gratitude and love for all we share and all they give.

To the astrologers I meet at conferences or online, and to the many astrologers, who practice quietly at kitchen tables around the world. We are all part of one community. We are all family, and to you I send my most heartfelt gratitude and encouragement. It is a path of absolute dedication to a voice of inner authority within that leads us to this practice. As much as you give, as much as the rewards are there.

Credits

Cover Art and Design: Yaviz Basalamah

Astrology Glyphs and Exercise Silhouette images curtesy of Pixabay

Anatomical Man, Très Riches Heures du Duc de Berry, Limbourg Brothers c. 1402- 1416

Anterior and Posterior Views of Muscles, Version 8.25 from the Textbook OpenStax, Anatomy and Physiology, Published May 18, 2016

Plato's Timaeus c.360 BC

French Vanity Fair named Nadiya Shah one of the top 12 astrologers on the planet, crowning her a pioneer in video astrology. She is an Internationally Syndicated Astrologer, Author, Media Personality, and is one of the few people in the world to hold an M.A. in the Cultural Study of Cosmology and Divination, from the University of Kent, United Kingdom.

Her School *Synchronicity University* teaches astrology online and worldwide. Nadiya's wildly popular Youtube channel, *nadiyashahdotcom*, is one of the most watched Astrology channels in the world.

The Meditations in this book are available as Guided Mediations in audio format on Nadiya's website.

Visit Nadiya's website at:

NadiyaShah.com

Made in the USA
Columbia, SC
02 March 2020